How to
Succeed
with
People

How to Succeed with People

Stephen R. Covey

Deseret Book Company   Salt Lake City, Utah 1979

Library of Congress No. 78-156812
SBN No. 87747-439-7

LITHOGRAPHED BY

DESERET NEWS PRESS

IN THE UNITED STATES OF AMERICA

Preface

> For this is the Journey that men make;
> to find themselves. If they fail in this it
> matters little whatever else they may
> achieve: Money, Fame, Revenge. When
> they end the journey, they can throw
> all of these things into a bin marked
> "ASHES." They mean nothing. But if
> one has found that he has within him
> a divine soul, if he has discovered the
> principles upon which the fulfillment
> of that soul is based, and if he imple-
> ments those principles, then he has a
> mansion within which he can live with
> dignity and joy each day of his life.*

This book includes a majority of the articles prepared originally for a column under the same title, "How To Succeed With People," for the Church News Section of the Deseret News.

Nothing causes a person to crystallize and capture his own experiences and thinking quite like writing short subject essays! I feel grateful and hope they also prove genuinely helpful to others.

The organization of this book into five sections is for convenience, although the subjects are interrelated with each other and spring from common underlying roots and principles.

As a preface to these short essays perhaps the following divine counsel well capsulizes the basic principles on which a soul is fulfilled.

> "Search diligently, pray always, and be
> believing, and all things shall work to-
> gether for your good, if ye walk uprightly
> and remember the covenant where-
> with ye have covenanted one with
> another."

—D&C 90:24

STEPHEN R. COVEY

*Quoted from Reed Bradford, paraphrasing James Michener.

To my parents, whose love, interest, and gentle
ways have been a constant source of
emotional support and spiritual encouragement

Table of Contents

I
SELF

1

Take Time to Sharpen the Saw

If you were guaranteed that by using one hour a day in a particular way you would both enjoy and be more productive in the other twenty-three hours, would you do it? "Of course I would," you say.

But would you? You should, because it's literally true and can be proven by any individual willing to give it a fair trial.

The purpose and content of this one hour is to sharpen our three instruments—our body, our mind, and our spirit. It takes time and effort to sharpen them, but this time is negligible compared to the time (and nerves) saved.

Sometimes when we are terribly busy and under a lot of pressure, with many commitments and involvements, we become neglectful of the only instruments or tools we have to do our work. We think we haven't time to consider them. In a sense we are literally saying, "I am too busy sawing to take time to sharpen the saw."

I suggest three activities for this hour: one physical, one mental, one spiritual.

First, physical exercise.

I won't take time to repeat all the obvious benefits of physical exercise but will only underscore the well-attested fact that a program of regular exercise increases one's efficiency in every facet of life, including the depth and restfulness of sleep. And the time taken can be minimal; just a few minutes of calisthenics and running in place in one's room or jogging around the yard or block is often sufficient. Exercising doesn't *take* time. It *saves* time. Still, few consistently do it.

Second, planning.

Many of us feel that no matter how hard we apply ourselves or how we reorganize our time, we still have the feeling of being behind, of being pushed and pressured, of having more things to do than we can satisfactorily handle.

Sometimes the answer is found in working longer and harder, but often the real key is in working smarter.

To work smarter requires planning. Planning is creative thinking. It involves analyzing the needs of situations, setting goals or objectives, and determining a course of action in achieving them.

Such hard mental work takes a little time, but without it we become bogged down in detail and trivia, pushed here and there, responding only to the immediate pressures, to the demands and wants of others, to symptoms rather than to the causes of problems and the real needs of situations. Goethe put it this way: "Things which matter most must never be at the mercy of things which matter least." Careful planning helps us maintain a sense of perspective, of purpose, and of ordered priorities.

The more rushed we are, the more time we better spend planning our time and actions. Otherwise we become like the frantic driver who is too much in a hurry to go two miles out of his way to take the freeway and who then proceeds to burn himself up, rushing, then cussing every red light and every slowpoke on the old highway.

Third, meditation, scripture study, and prayer.

Interwoven with planning is the effort to provide nourishment for the spirit, which we are all in constant need of as much as we need food for the body.

Prayerfully studying God's word in the scriptures and listening, through quiet meditation, to the still small voice within will result in a sense of eternal perspective, of divine need and purpose. It will also chasten, enlighten, and motivate, and is excellent preparation for secret prayer. Such prayer, offered from a sincere heart, is a perfect time for recommitment, for promising to obey the laws upon which the blessings requested are predicated. ". . . thy vows shall be offered up in righteousness on all days and at all times. . . ." (D&C 59:11.)

The great reformer Martin Luther understood this principle: "I've got so much to do today I'll need to spend another hour on my knees." To him prayer was not a mechanical duty but rather a source of power in releasing and multiplying his energies, by renewing an alliance with One who alone could make him equal to the day's tasks.

To use a physical analogy, such an alliance that is continually renewed in prayer is comparable to a farmer's using a powerful harvesting machine as contrasted to his neighbor's doing it all by hand because he couldn't "afford the time or money or bother" to rent one.

These three activities need not take more than one hour a day, but they will immeasurably influence the quality of the other twenty-three, for we are working upon the roots of both our problems and our successes. A sharp saw always cuts faster and better, and we must never be too busy to sharpen ours.

2

Be Strong in Hard Moments

There are certain moments in every person's day that, if excellently used, will determine the direction and quality of all the other moments. These certain moments are few in number—sometimes very few. They are necessarily hard moments, testing moments.

Missionary work illustrates this well. There are generally three crucial moments in a missionary's day, and if he can be strong or true in these three hard moments, everything else tends to fall into place successfully.

These three moments are (1) getting up at 6:00 A.M.; (2) the initial moment of contacting; and (3) the moment when he gets an investigator to make a commitment.

1. The time of 6:00 A.M. in the schedule of missionary life symbolizes mastery over the flesh. Mind over mattress. If a missionary can overcome the pull of the flesh in the beginning moment of his day—often his hardest moment— he can overcome the lesser moments.

2. Initial contacting of new people takes initiative and courage. If the missionary will plunge into it at the appointed hour, refusing to shrink from it by doing easier things, he will develop power reserves to do many other hard things well.

3. Being strong, with love, in committing investigators to obey gospel laws, tests and nurtures both the emotional

and the spiritual roots of the missionary. Conducting safe but powerless philosophical gospel discussions takes little strength or courage.

Isn't it also true that if we, as parents or students, are courageous in just a few hard things each day, all else will fall into place? Sounds simple, I know, but I believe the answer is yes. The proof is in the doing, and this is not simple.

Certainly these things vary with each individual. Each must examine himself to find the few crucial daily moments that determine so much else.

Consider three things, three hard moments that are so basic and so determining for so many.

First, getting up in the morning when we know we should.

Always being a few minutes behind in our work is a kind of emotional mortgage on the day. Tyrannized by the clock, we interpret almost every event selfishly. We fret and worry. We become overly impatient with weakness and mistakes, our own as well as those of others. Interruptions and inconveniences are resented. No time for kindness, for listening, for extra service. The spirit of rushing and hurrying destroys a good family spirit.

The consequences of a few minutes more sleep are often so exhausting!

Second, making reconciliation to the Lord's will.

To reconcile means to bring together, to unite, to bring back into harmony and friendship. If we are not careful to daily drink of the "living waters," we can easily and slowly become strangers to the Lord and his ways and to our own divine identity and purpose. We learn his ways from prayerfully searching the scriptures. Listening then to the still small voice of conscience and then committing in secret prayer to obey its promptings that day complete this reconciliation.

Third, to control our tongue.

To not say the unkind or critical thing, particularly when provoked and/or fatigued, is a supreme kind of self-mastery.

President McKay taught, "Never must there be expressed in a Latter-day Saint home an oath, a condemnatory term, an expression of anger or jealousy or hatred. Control it! Do not express it! You do what you can to produce peace and harmony no matter what you may suffer."

As in all things, the Savior is again the perfect model of this principle. Everything culminated in his supreme tests at Gethsemane and Calvary. We are all beneficiaries of his being strong and true in that transcendent moment of eternity.

To simply understand the pervasive power of a few moments in a day is highly motivating in itself, in marshaling and unifying our will, our nerve, and our energy.

Someone rightly defined courage as the quality of every quality at its highest testing point.

3

Work on the Roots

What would you think if a person were to construct a dam, for aesthetic reasons, on a mountain top instead of the base of a canyon?

Or what would you think if one were to attempt to build an internal combustion engine on the principle that gases contract when heated?

In either case you would answer that the individuals were ignoring basic natural laws: gravity and expansion of gas when heated. Neither the dam nor the engine would work, regardless of how beautifully located or well constructed.

These two farfetched examples illustrate a simple point: to make things work we must understand and work with, not against, the nature of things.

Actually, these examples are not so farfetched after all. The history of every field of science gives abundant evidence of how new scientific discoveries upturn and make obsolete many well-established theories and practices. Many of the great scientific breakthroughs have been breakwiths.

Take the applied science of medicine as another example. In tribal days witch doctoring was the accepted thing. The natives thought they understood the nature of things —that the evil spirits caused disease and that the witch doctor possessed magical powers. To them, these ideas or assumptions were facts. To us today these assumptions are superstitions, born of ignorance and fear. Pure research into the nature of things has enabled applied medical science to work seeming miracles, extending our life-span twice that of our forebears several generations ago.

This thinking has direct application to the fields of human behavior, such as family relations, communications, and leadership, for, as with the physical and medical science analogies, if our theories of reality (and we are all acting on them) aren't accurate, we're in trouble.

The vital question, therefore, is: What is the nature of things regarding man and his relationships?

Our answers come from basically two sources: man's discoveries and God's revelations. If these two ever seem to conflict, revelations must take precedence, for the tools of science are finite and cannot refute or explain the infinite.

To deny or to ignore what has been revealed about man doesn't change the nature of things one bit! It simply becomes another case of witch doctoring.

The following basic realities about man have been revealed and have profound, far-reaching consequences in our discussions of human relations.

1. Man is an immortal spirit, clothed in a physical body.

2. His growth and development are governed by spiritual and moral laws.

3. Through disobedience to those laws, man becomes insecure and alienated from himself, from his Creator, and from his fellowmen.

4. By obedience to the laws and ordinances of the gospel, through the atonement of Christ, man becomes secure and unified within himself, with his Creator, and with his fellowmen.

Based on the above analysis, I offer two personal convictions.

First, the real nature of our problems is spiritual.

That is, the roots of our problems lie in our disobeying natural laws—knowingly or unknowingly.

Examine any problems you face from that standpoint, whether family finances, relationship breakdowns between husband and wife or parent and child, fear of failure, obesity, confusion in making decisions, despair over world conditions, or whatever.

Start with the surface complaint and ask what caused it. Then ask what caused that and what caused that and so on. Such causal-chain thinking will eventually lead back to show either a lack of understanding of reality (life's purpose, man's nature, the governing laws) or a lack of commitment and self-discipline to live accordingly —thus procrastination, impatience, overeating, selfishness, etc.

Notice how most of these discussions eventually return to the fundamental principles of understanding or commitment or discipline, expressed in various ways.

Second, the basic solution to our problems also lies within ourselves. We can't escape the nature of things. Like it or not, realize it or not, God's authority is in us. That is, his nature, his laws, and our conscience.

It's futile to fight our battles on the wrong battlefields. We must work on causes, not symptoms. Taking aspirin for a headache won't eliminate future headaches.

The spiritual resources available to us are fathomless and possess infinite wisdom and power. But the initiative, the first step, lies with us.

"For every thousand hacking at the leaves of evil, there is one striking at the root." (Thoreau.)

4

The Power of Self-Understanding

One of the principal reasons we have a hard time understanding others is because we lack understanding of ourselves.

A little thinking will reveal why this is so. The very tool we use to understand another is within us, and if we are confused about ourselves—the lens we look through—obviously, inevitably, we will also be cloudy about others.

In light of this idea, study the following story of a woman who came to better understand her family problems and who changed her life through gaining precious insights about herself and acting on them.

"For years and years I fought with my children and they fought with each other. I was constantly judging and criticizing and scolding.

"I knew something had to be done. But I didn't know what. I did know my incessant critical nagging was hurting their self-esteem and the whole spirit of our home, causing much of the contention.

"Again and again I would resolve and try to change. And just as often I would fall back. Then I'd feel awful—guilty—angry with myself. I hated myself, and as I saw my own weaknesses in my children's behavior, I took out my self-anger on them. Then I'd feel more guilty, and the more guilt I felt the more anger I expressed.

"Eventually I decided to make my problems a matter of sustained and specific and earnest prayer. Gradually I came to two insights about my real motives and reasons for my negative critical behavior.

"First, I came to see more clearly the impact of my own childhood home experiences. Our home was broken in almost every way and eventually ended in divorce. I can't ever remember seeing my parents talk through their problems and differences. They would either argue and fight or they'd angrily separate. The silent treatment —sometimes for days.

"So when I had to deal with the same issues and problems with my own family, I had no model or example to follow. I really didn't know what to do. Instead of finding a model or fighting it through within myself, I'd take out my confusion and frustration on the kids. And yet, as much as I didn't like it, I found myself dealing with my children just as my parents did with us.

"One more immensely helpful self-insight came to me. I was trying to win, to wrest social approval out of my own children's behavior. Because I was constantly fearful of being embarrassed, I constantly instructed and threatened and bribed and manipulated to get my kids to behave—all so others would think well of me.

"I could then see, in my own hunger for approval, that I was shielding my own children from growth and responsibility. I was helping cause the very thing I feared the most—irresponsible behavior."

I asked this woman how these two self-insights helped her.

She answered, "They've made all the difference in the world. I now realize I have to conquer my own problems within myself instead of taking them out on others.

"My unhappy, confused childhood inclined me to be negative but it didn't force me. I still had my agency. I could choose to respond differently. It was futile to blame my parents or my circumstances.

"Oh, it was hard to admit this to myself—very hard!

I struggled with years of accumulated pride. But once I swallowed the bitter pill, I had a marvelously free feeling. I was in control. I could choose a better way. I was responsible for myself.

"I've now learned to retire frequently to myself and win my own battles privately, to get my motives straight. And now when I get into a frustrating situation I stop. I pause. I back away from impulsively speaking or striking out. I try for perspective and control. Sometimes I simply go alone and struggle the thing through on my own. I find new models, new examples to follow, the perfect one being the Savior. The scriptures and prayer have helped greatly."

Look at the miracles these two self-insights produced! This woman's new understanding of herself taught her how to use it to control herself. It also inspired her to take responsibility for her own behavior and attitudes, for both her actions and her reactions.

We simply do not win our own battles on someone else's battlefield.

"The greatest battles of life are fought out daily in the silent chambers of the soul." (David O. McKay.)

Private victories precede public victories.

5

Patience: Its Nature and Its Growth

Many admit to being impatient. "I have some virtues but patience isn't one of them. I wish I could develop more patience," we say.

Not knowing exactly how to develop patience, we generally forget about it and go about our lives in the spirit of rush and hurry, critical of the slowness and weaknesses of others. Then, in times of stress, particularly around loved ones, our impatient mood surfaces and our temper flashes. We may say something we don't really mean or intend to say—all out of proportion to reality.

Or we may become sullen, slowly burning inside and communicating through emotion and attitude, rather than words, eloquent messages of criticalness, judgment, and rejection. Our harvest is bitter: hurt feelings, strained relationships, little growth. Again seeing the fruits of our impatience, we repeat, "I wish I were more patient," almost as if this were a quirk of our nature we could do nothing about.

Let's examine two questions: What is patience? and How can we develop it?

1. Notice how literally patience is the practical expression of faith, hope, wisdom, and love. First, patience is not a passive virtue as some think. Patience is extremely active emotionally.

For instance, what kind of father would slap or criticize or otherwise punish his infant son when he totters and falls while learning to walk? Why is this extreme foolishness so self-evident to us? Because we all know that falling is part of learning to walk. We know if we punish falling, the boy will stop trying. Unless he tries he'll never learn to walk. He'll just crawl.

This simple analogy can be extended to include all learning and development. Patience accepts the reality of life that in all things there is a process, a step one, step two, step three process that cannot be ignored or bypassed.

Faith embodies patience. It is a contradiction for someone to think or feel he has faith but lacks patience. Faith deals with the unseen. The father helps and encourages his tottering son to walk. Why? Because of what he sees? No, for he sees only falling. He does it because of what he does not see, because of what he believes. He believes in his son's potential to walk and he acts accordingly. That's faith. It's also hope. That's why he patiently encourages and waits.

Patience obviously, therefore, is not indifference, is not sullen endurance, is not a matter of doing nothing. Patience is faith in action. Patience is emotional diligence.

Consider the scriptural definition of patience: long-suffering. We suffer inside when we want something now and can't have it. We suffer inside when we have to wait for someone to bungle through the learning process to do their job. "It's easier to do it myself," we reason. We suffer inside when the results we want, and are judged by, require the willing cooperation of those who either don't know how or don't care.

The willingness to suffer inside so others can grow takes love. As we become aware of our suffering, we learn about ourselves and our own motives and weaknesses. Knowledge of ourselves and life's processes, combined with self-restraint, produces the sense and ability to know when to do what. This is wisdom.

What a small price such long-suffering is for such

huge gains! "Patience is bitter but its fruit is sweet." (Rousseau.)

2. The development of patience is akin to the development of one's body or muscles through resistance exercises. In exercising, a point is reached when the strain on the muscle causes its fiber to rupture. Then when nature repairs the broken fiber, she overcompensates and the muscle grows in strength, elasticity, and power.

Similarly, there are three aspects in the development of patience fiber.

First, purpose and a commitment to it. Those who would like more patience but lack a strong desire and sense of purpose (the *way* of it) will be easily uprooted under the first strain.

Second, resistance. Patience is not developed as knowledge is acquired from books, but only under testing and strain. Life provides abundant opportunities to practice patience—to stretch the emotional fiber—from waiting for a late person or plane to listening quietly to your child's feelings and experiences when other things are pressing. Cheerfully bearing the little annoyances and trials of every day builds and strengthens the emotional fiber for times of real stress and calamity.

Third, be patient with the development of patience itself. Otherwise, you'll give up on both the effort and yourself. The roots of impatience lie in other weaknesses and habits and are not pulled up without some pain and consistent effort through time. Have faith in your own unseen potential.

6

Three Processes: Knowing, Choosing, Doing

The most spectacular and celebrated—and certainly the most involving—technical achievement of all time was the Apollo 11 moon trip. How ironic to witness such herculean feats while fighting hot and cold wars all around this globe. As one observer put it, "We are technical giants and moral pigmies."

Why? Why such a massive gap between our technical and our human relationship achievements? Many think it is because the physical sciences have outstripped the social sciences and therefore we need to pour more of our energies and resources into the study of how to improve human relationships. I believe this idea is not only false but highly misleading.

If we include the teachings of the Lord, the social or human behavior sciences are far ahead of the physical sciences. The basic principles and laws given have never been improved upon or changed since Adam, the first man. Founded on the Ten Commandments, they move to the Golden Rule and the laws of love, repentance, and forgiveness.

This is not so with the physical sciences. Much that was taught as scientific fact in school years ago is discarded today. Many of the great "breakthroughs" were "breakwiths."

Where, then, is the lag? In doing. In applying. The applied social sciences lag far behind the applied physical sciences.

Each of us can look about our own lives to see the evidence and the origin of this gap between knowing and doing. Few of us "do" as well as we "know." Why is this so? I suggest the answer lies in our skipping or neglecting a fundamental connecting step or link between what we know and what we do. This is the step or process of choosing.

Choosing means to pause and stand back for perspective, to think deeply, and then to decide our own actions and reactions. Choosing means to accept responsibility for ourselves and our attitudes, to refuse to blame others or circumstances.

Choosing, then, means to commit ourselves strongly to that which we decide to do. This committing process often involves a real internal struggle, ultimately between competing motives or between conflicting concepts of ourselves.

This choosing (deciding and committing) step can break the binding power of habits if enough effort goes into it. This is more than strong resolution or sheer will-power. Many exert great willpower to overcome a fault or habit or to accomplish an important project, but they don't inwardly believe they will really succeed. They see themselves, perhaps unconsciously, as incapable or unworthy of success. They've failed before—they'll fail again. So before the doing process begins, they are already defeated. Private defeats precede public defeats.

This choosing process, therefore, also involves "belief power" (meaning great mental exertion)—seeing and imagining and feeling ourselves successfully doing what we desire to. Such a believing process welds the conscious and the unconscious forces together.

We have all experienced something powerful "connect" within ourselves once we made our mind up on a matter. We simply knew we could and would do it. And we did it. The private victory preceded the public victory.

In this choosing opportunity rests man's free agency—his supreme unique gift—and his accountability. Through it, man alone can use and build on the accumulated knowledge of the ages. No animal can do this. Through it, man alone can break with the past, even deeply imbedded habits, and determine his own future. No animal can do this. Deterministic philosophy—the idea that biological heritage and/or social environment sets or determines man's character and conduct—is animal psychology.

But unless we realize both our free agency and our power to choose and then use them wisely, our actions will be determined by the conditions, within and without, of our lives.

Look at it this way. Unless the choosing gear connects knowing to doing, we will still be connected to old habit gears and/or to the gears of others and of circumstances.

This choosing process takes time and great mental and spiritual exertion. Prayer and ordinance work can serve this purpose magnificently and release great powers, within and without. We'll do what we know we should if we regularly covenant deep enough to do so.

7

Distinguish Between Person and Performance

Parents, teachers, and leaders frequently bemoan the power that acceptance and popularity by the peer group have over their youth. "What can we do to decrease its influence and increase our own?" they plead.

There is, I believe, a common denominator behind much of the behavior of youth, an understanding of which is immensely helpful in dealing with them. It has to do with what is the primary source of their security or sense of worth.

Consider two terms—intrinsic and extrinsic—and the subsequent reasons. *First, intrinsic.* This means that one's primary source of security or sense of worth lies within. One has worth apart from his performance and apart from others' opinions of him. He feels deep inside, without having to think about it, "I'm good. I'm of worth, in and of myself."

Such a person possesses the inner strength and courage to act on what he knows is right regardless of popularity. In his own eyes he is somebody and stands for something, so social pressure, even rejection, doesn't control him or "wipe him out."

Second, extrinsic. This means that one's primary sense of worth and value lies outside himself, particularly in the opinion of other people.

Again, it isn't so much an intellectual matter as it is emotional. This person may think "I am a child of God" but not feel it. His sense of goodness lies almost entirely in the good he does, not in the good he is.

Consequently, lacking security within, he seeks it without—sometimes almost desperately in trying to be all things to all people.

Policed by the reactions of others, he's torn inside as he finds everyone expects different things: "My parents expect this, the Church that, and my friends that." Confused and lonely, he often withdraws into a "safe" world of his own making.

Perhaps a more typical reaction pattern with many youth is to conform to the values and expectations of the group from which they seek acceptance and approval, and to rebel, to greater or lesser degrees, against their parents and their parents' values. The first outward manifestations of this rebellion to conformity may be dress and hair styles, language used, and defensive attitudes. It will often lead to other compromises—vulgarity, lying, cheating, stealing, and eventually smoking, drinking, drugs, unchastity. Then, of course, these perversions of life horribly compound and complicate both the root problems and the way back.

Our efforts to reach them, to reclaim them, are sometimes done in the very way (judging, moralizing) they interpret as rejection of them as persons, exalting again only the good they should do. This solidifies both their rebellious patterns and their present loyalties as the only source of their identity or sense of being a person, an individual.

In some way we need to communicate an understanding and acceptance of them as persons without approving or condoning their behavior. Although difficult to do, it can be done. Our youth want it more than they would dare tell us.

One of the basic early causes of extrinsic sense of worth is the widespread tendency at home and school and in society to compare one person with another and, most importantly, to emotionally reward (praise, warmth, love) and punish (impatience, displeasure, judgment, rejection) on the basis of that comparison.

Think this through carefully: when comparisons are habitual, when a person's worth and his performance are one and the same thing, gradually the source of worth moves out of him (intrinsic) and into someone else's opinion (extrinsic) of his performance. "She's our bright one." "He's the slow one." "He's smart but he just won't apply himself like his brother." "I just can't understand it at all—you should have done better than Susan." "Your grades are getting embarrassing to us, honey."

Such labels or definitions habitually given are soon believed and lived up to and emotionally accepted as part of a person's concept of self. "Of course I failed—'cause I'm a failure. Just ask anybody."

It is vital to distinguish between a person and his behavior or performance. While we need to disapprove of bad behavior and reward superior performance, we first need to communicate and help build in our young people a sense of intrinsic worth and goodness and esteem totally apart from these comparisons and judgments. Ironically, success in doing this will powerfully serve to inspire superior effort. It is a self-fulfilling prophecy.

The very power to understand the crucial distinction between person and performance and to communicate intrinsic worth to others flows naturally out of our own sense of intrinsic worth and value. Otherwise we will find ourselves wresting our own personal security from the performance of our youth and will therefore be unable to communicate intrinsic worth to them.

8

Eight Sources of Inner Security

When a person has a deep inner sense of personal worth, he is more effective in all phases of his life. He is also genuinely happy for the successes of others, feeling that nothing is being taken from him.

Consider eight different, although interrelated, sources of a deep sense of intrinsic worth and inner personal security. Carefully notice how the items emphasized, under each of the eight sources, deal with developing a sense of worth within each individual, rather than without, from opinions or comparisons.

First, the family.

One's emotional roots lie primarily in the unconditional love and regard that parents have for their children and for each other. Frequently, time is taken for each one for private visits and understanding. When one parent shows kindness, respect, and courtesy to the other parent, the children feel value is also given to them—intrinsic value.

Family councils are held. Each opinion is listened to, respected, and considered. There's an absence of comparing one against another, of arbitrary rule making, of inconsistent mood-of-the-moment disciplining. There's the presence of family prayer, family traditions, family goals, schedules, duties, limits, rules, rights, privileges, consistently firm and fair discipline, honoring of promises.

"There is beauty all around when there's love at home."

Second, church activity and service.

Condemning the sin, yet valuing the sinner, the Church places supreme value on the intrinsic worth of each individual. Whenever we reach outside ourselves in the Lord's pattern to serve another, we communicate value to him and receive value in return. Genuine involvement ("with real intent") in teaching, leading, ordinance work for the living or the dead, or merely attending and participating in the church climate yields a sense of individual worth and personal security.

Third, nature.

Nature is very life-affirming and bequeaths its silent strength to one who takes time to feel and to appreciate. To absorb ourself in the magnificent beauty of the mountains, to spend time at the beach or in any lovely natural setting, including our own backyard, brings an intrinsic sense of worth, if we take the time to be still and to meditate, to drink it all in.

Fourth, continuing education.

Education's main value does not lie in getting knowledge, much of which will be obsolete sooner or later. It certainly doesn't lie in credits earned or degrees conferred. These may open doors of opportunity, but only real competence will keep them open. In fact, in our rapidly changing world there is no "future," no economic security in any job or situation. The only real economic security lies within the person, in his competence and power to produce.

Education's main value lies in learning how to continually learn, how to think and to communicate, how to appreciate and to produce, how to adapt to changing realities without sacrificing changeless values. Result? An inner confidence in the basic ability to cope successfully with whatever life brings.

To keep informed and alive, adults need some kind of system that contains balance and substance and requires mental concentration and discipline—a reading program, discussion groups, a correspondence course, an education week, or whatever.

Children need to be encouraged to be conscientious on a daily basis in their school and homework. Value should be placed on their disciplined efforts and love of learning and creativity as well as on grades and other academic achievements. Youth really know inside how they're doing in school, in several important ways, far more than their teachers or parents do, and their own honest self-evaluations should be discussed and respected.

Fifth, anonymous service.

Whenever we do good for others when no one knows save God and us alone, our intrinsic sense of worth and respect increases. ". . . thy Father which seeth in secret himself shall reward thee openly." (Matt. 6:4.)

Sixth, daily work.

Doing ordinary everyday work well brings its own rewards to each person. But doing it excellently, going the second mile, doing something creative and unique multiplies those intrinsic rewards. Two activities in work will influence results the most: planning and honest two-way communication with key people. A personal sense of self-mastery is internally more rewarding than any form of economic or social reward.

Seventh, a spiritually rich private life.

Daily and weekly immersion in gospel teachings, in the scriptures, in private worship, in meditation and prayer releases enormous resources within us of peace and serenity, understanding and courage. The scriptures teach that we will abide in the Lord's love—the perfect source of divine definition of self—if we abide in his word.

Eighth, integrity.

When we live true to the light and truth we have received, we will receive more light and truth. If we are untrue to that light (our conscience), we experience disunity and insecurity within. Then, unless we repent, this internal warring will breed guilt, anger, and defensiveness, and will undermine both our resolve and our capacity to tap the other seven sources of personal security.

The key is to be a doer, not just a hearer; to be a light, not a judge of the darkness.

9

True Freedom Lies Within

The ultimate, perhaps the last, freedom is the right and power to decide within how anybody or anything outside ourself will affect us. Many people are simply unaware they have this capacity, this freedom.

During a speech on this subject once a woman in the audience literally lit up. She seemed so ecstatic and radiant she could hardly contain herself. At the conclusion of the talk I went to her and asked what had happened. She answered, "You have no idea what the point on attitude control means to me. You see, I have been a full-time nurse for over three years to the most miserable, ungrateful, crotchety old man you can imagine. But up until tonight I have been feeling how miserable he has made my life. Tonight I have come to realize that I have chosen to be miserable. He hasn't made me miserable. I have chosen to respond to his behavior in that way. This is a bitter pill to swallow. But the thing that really hit home to me was the thought that since I had freely chosen the negative response to a negative situation, I have the freedom to choose otherwise. No longer will he control my disposition. I will control it."

Dr. Viktor E. Frankl, a Jewish Austrian psychotherapist, was imprisoned in various concentration camps in Germany during the second world war. His parents, his brother, and his wife died in the camps or were sent to the gas ovens. Except for his sister, his entire family perished in these camps. He was stripped of all his possessions. He suffered torture and innumerable indignities. He never knew from one moment to the next if his path would lead to the gas chambers or the ovens, or if he would be among the "saved" who would remove the bodies or shovel out the ashes of those so fated.

One day, alone in a small room, stripped naked, he began to become aware of the last freedom. It was the only freedom, he said, they could not take from him: he could decide within himself how all of this was going to affect him. He proceeded to act upon this awareness. It grew and grew through mental concentration and self-discipline until he acquired unusual controls within himself. He became an inspiration to those around him, even to the guards. He helped others find meaning in their suffering and dignity in their prison existence.

The essence of the Savior's life and teachings deals with internal freedom or control: turn the other cheek, go the second mile, "pray for those who curse you," "love your enemies," etc. The Lord told the Prophet Joseph Smith that his suffering "shall give thee experience, and shall be for thy good." This very kind of internal attitude control, this freedom, provides the most powerful evidence of overcoming the world and of one's true discipleship to the Son of God.

The world's doctrine of determinism links stimulus and response together as inseparable. However, once we are aware that we can decide within ourself what our response will be to a given stimulus (environment or person), they become separated. This very awareness becomes the embryo of our freedom. If we then continue to act on that awareness by overcoming evil with good, by returning cheerfulness in the face of gloom and pessimism, patience toward the impatient, kindness to the unkind, our internal freedom will continue to grow and grow. It is exactly because we have this freedom that we are responsible and will be held responsible by its author, our Creator.

27

For our purpose here, let us define liberty as the opportunity in life to choose between alternatives and freedom as the internal power or capacity to choose between alternatives. In this sense Dr. Frankl had freedom but not liberty. Similarly we may have liberty (opportunity) but not freedom (power), perhaps because of our addiction to the habit of gratifying an appetite or passion.

For instance, in sports, a golfer studies each situation and uses the appropriate club. He has freedom (developed power). But if he only knows how to use one club, although he could choose others, he has no power (freedom).

So in our relations with others. If we are addicted to interpret every situation in terms of our own convenience or pleasure or ego and then become upset or angry when things don't go our way, we truly are slaves, even as we proclaim our freedom to do our "own thing."

Therefore, freedom is responsible self-discipline, the opposite of license. We act from divine principles and conscience within rather than react to changing and fickle values and realities without.

10

Step-by-Step Victory Over Self

Most relationship problems stem from personal problems, in at least two distinct ways.

First is the way we take out our guilt on others. When we are not true to our conscience, we are at war with ourselves. Rather than repenting, the natural tendency is to take that war out on others. We do it when we find their weakness, the mote in their eye, and thus can momentarily forget the beam in our own—mote-beam sickness.

Much of the arguing, contending, and criticizing in family circles follows a combination of low achievement and high fatigue. As one put it, "When I don't feel good about myself, you better watch out!"

The second kind of personal problem is interwoven with the first and perhaps is its prime cause—a lack of self-discipline. When we are controlled by our appetites and passions, we inevitably have relationship problems. All it takes is a time of stress and/or fatigue to uproot our best intentions.

The following true story is one clear illustration of how relationships inevitably deteriorate through a lack of self-discipline and how they can be made beautiful by growth in self-discipline, which I'm defining here as the ability to make and keep promises.

It involves an undisciplined missionary who pleaded with his mission president for a transfer from his companion, claiming, "We just can't get along." The president counseled him that he could learn to get along if he would only hold his tongue, serve his companion, and obey true principles of self-control, of love and service. The missionary resolved to do so but his hair-trigger temper gripped him more than his resolve. As with many, he had the habit of making and breaking resolutions.

Again and again he requested a transfer, once saying, "I'm afraid of what I might do if I really lost my temper." And again and again his president would commit him to principles of self-control, of love and service. Nothing seemed to take until one day the leader realized that, in a sense, he was teaching him to run before he could walk, for his reactions and emotions were controlled far more by the habits and appetites of his flesh and the temper of his spleen than by the momentary sincerity of his resolves.

If hungry, he'd eat, and eat, and eat. If sleepy, he'd sleep—even in meetings. If upset, he'd show it. If angry, he'd express it. Yet, when he felt fine, he was ever so sweet and pleasant and ever so repentant and resolved. He merely took the course of least resistance in each situation.

So, one day, after weeks of counseling, the leader asked the missionary to promise to get up at 5:55 A.M. for one month.

"I can't understand it," he retorted. "I asked you to help me with my relationship problem and you ask me to get up at 5:55."

"Elder, how can you possibly control and direct your emotions until you have more control of the very instrument through which you express your emotions—your body? Let's begin at the first step and take one at a time. Will you get up at 5:55 for one full month?"

"I'm not sure I can."

"Then don't promise to. Will you for a week?"

"I will," he answered.

A week later: "Did you keep your promise?"

"I did."

"Congratulations! Now let's take step two. Will you study alone and with your companion for two and one half hours every morning for a week?"

"I can't. My mind jumps all around the place."

"Will you just sit there for two and a half hours and try?"

"I will."

He did it. Week by week, month by month, he made and kept promises. Little by little, line upon line, he grew in self-mastery, in integrity, in spirituality. His relationships with others, even with difficult persons, were magnificent, and he became one of the most powerful and effective and respected missionary leaders in the field. Through making and keeping small resolves, small promises, he had won a victory over himself. He learned the hard way that "the body is a good servant but a bad master."

There are several principles of personal growth and human relations here. Consider five, which build on each other.

1. We must never make a promise we will not keep.

2. To grow we must make promises (resolutions, commitments, oaths, covenants) to do better, to be better.

3. We must use self-knowledge and be very careful and selective about the promises we make, for all things must be done in order (in the right sequence).

4. Our ability to make and keep promises is the measure of our faith in ourselves and of our integrity.

5. This integrity, or self-mastery, is also basic to our faith in God, for his promises to us are conditioned on our keeping our promises to him.

Therefore, in one sense, the whole system of relationships—human and divine—is based on a step-by-step victory over self.

"A 1,000-mile journey begins with a single step."

II

RELATIONSHIPS

How to Influence Others

The accompanying diagram shows how one can effectively influence others. It will help to refer to it as you consider the subsequent reasoning together with the real human influence problems and challenges you face.

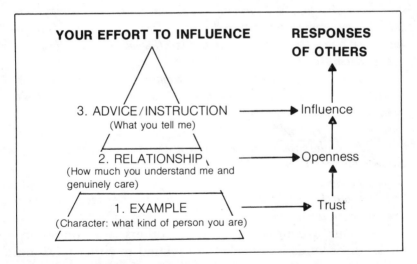

First, note the three basic interrelated phases or levels: (1) example, (2) relationship, and (3) advice/instruction. To illustrate how each phase necessarily builds on the other, assume for a moment I am the person—your spouse or child or worker or boss or neighbor or whoever—you are attempting to influence, perhaps after some past failure to do so.

1. *"The key and foundation to your influence with me is your example, your actual conduct,"* I begin. *"Your example flows naturally out of your character or the kind of a person you truly are, not what others say you are or what you may want me to think you are; it is evidenced in how I actually experience you.*

"Your essential character is constantly radiating, communicating. From it in the long run, I come to instinctively trust or distrust you and your efforts with me. It is a matter of degree, of course.

"If your life runs hot and cold, if you're both caustic and kind and, above all, if your private performance doesn't square with your public performance, it's very hard for me to open up with you. Then as much as I may want and even need to receive your love and influence, I don't feel safe enough to expose my opinions and experiences and my tender feelings. Who knows what will happen? I've been hurt before and I'm not going to chance it again."

2. *"But unless I open up with you, unless you understand me and my unique situation and feelings, you won't know how to advise or counsel me. What you say is all good and fine, but you see, it doesn't quite pertain to me.*

"You say you care about and appreciate me. (Oh, how I wish I could believe that!) But how could you appreciate when you don't even understand? Just words. I can't trust words. If you would just try to understand . . ."

3. *"Unless you're influenced by my uniqueness, I'm not going to be influenced by your advice. I'm too angry and defensive—perhaps I'm too guilty and afraid—to be influenced, even though inside I know I need what you have to tell me. Besides, you don't even practice what you preach."*

In our attempts to influence others, we commonly make three kinds of mistakes, all related to either ignoring or shortcutting these same three intertwined phases of influence.

First, we try to tell or advise others before we have established any understanding relationship, any real communication. Our advice, however sound, will generally not be received until the feeling is good. I suggest the supreme skill needed here is empathy.

Second, we try to build or rebuild a relationship without making any fundamental change in our conduct or attitude. If our example is pockmarked with inconsistency and insincerity, no amount of win-friends-influence-people technique will work. As Emerson so aptly put it, "What you are shouts so loudly in my ears I can't hear what you say."

Third, we assume that a good example and a good relationship are sufficient, that we don't need to explicitly teach the "shoulds" of life. If this were true, we would need neither weekday school nor Sunday School.

We need to teach the words of life and of eternal life by both example and precept. We need to give the vision and to testify of it. Just as vision without love contains no motivation, so also love without vision contains no goals, no guidelines, no standards, no lifting power.

And realistically we need to focus others' attention on our Lord and Savior, the perfect exemplar, so as to gradually lessen their dependency on our imperfect examples (as was evidenced in the above monologue). As "the Way, the Life, and the Truth," he simultaneously embodies and integrates all three levels and is the perfect source and model of influence.

12

Give Positive Experiences

One of the main reasons behind communication break-downs is because the people involved interpret the same event differently. Their different natures and different background experiences condition them to do so. If they then interact without taking into account why they see things differently, they begin to judge each other.

This judging tears at the relationship, compounding the communication breakdown and spawning longer-term personality conflicts.

For instance, take as small a thing as a difference in room temperature. The thermostat on the wall clearly registers 75 degrees. One complains "It's too hot," and opens the windows; the other complains "It's too cold," and closes them.

Who is right? Is it too hot or too cold? The fact is they are both right.

Can two people disagree and both be right? Obviously yes. Each is right from his own point of view. And probably each will respect this fact and either stop complaining or make a compromise satisfactory to both.

But what if they tried to prove each other wrong, saying such things as, "Too hot? Are you crazy? I'm freezing!"

Judging another's sanity or sincerity is a personal

attack and creates new and different relationship problems that are far more difficult to solve.

When we apply this same reasoning to the sense of seeing or to the sense of hearing, we open up a fruitful understanding of human problems.

We do this in the classroom with some simple pictures. First, we briefly show a picture of a young girl to one group and a picture of an old lady to another group. This first experience conditions how they will see and interpret the next experience. We then show both groups a composite picture, containing the outlines of both the young girl and the old woman. Finally, we ask them what they see and watch them interact with each other.

Several things inevitably happen. First, with few exceptions, they see as they were conditioned to—one group asserting "She's a young woman," and the other group answering "No, she's an old woman." Second, they begin to argue and frequently end in personally attacking either the judgment or the sincerity of the other. One says, "Don't put me on. You can see that wrinkled face and haggard old look just as well as I can!" The other answers, "Wrinkled face! What's wrong with you? She's lovely, young, and petite!" As each grows defensive he becomes even more convinced that "I'm right and you're wrong."

One person will eventually come to see another's point of view by first assuming that the other is sincere and then seeking to understand through asking and listening rather than telling and judging. Gradually, through respectful communication, almost everyone comes to see both points of view, usually with an "Oh! I see it!" Yet, I have students to this day who cannot. They invested so much ego in their defense as to freeze their initial perception or point of view.

The accompanying diagram attempts to summarize this most useful learning, which is applicable to every area of life, particularly the family.

While referring to the diagram, consider three implications:

1. Center blocks: Experiences tend to condition how

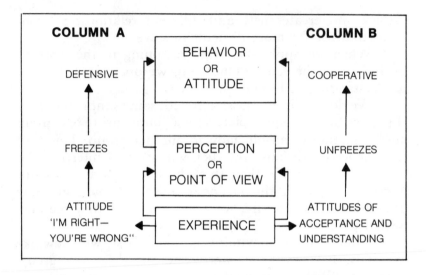

we perceive, and we behave accordingly—like looking at life through a very private lens or filter.

2. Column A: When we try to change another's behavior or attitude by telling and by judging ("I'm right—you're wrong"), we ignore implication No. 1 and thus give an experience that tends to freeze or reinforce his intial perception and also to increase his defensiveness.

3. Column B: When we assume the other is right from his point of view (for he is!) and then try to understand his point of view by asking questions and respectfully listening, we give an experience that encourages him to become open and cooperative.

In short, since people trust their own experiences, we had better give positive ones if we wish to influence them.

13

Assume the Best of Others

In human relations there is one attitude that continuously produces good fruit. It is the attitude of assuming good faith. This means to assume the best of others, to assume that they want to do well, that they mean to do well.

By acting on the assumption others are trying to do their best as they see it, though perhaps not as you see it, you can exert a powerful influence in bringing out the best in them. And vice versa.

Let me illustrate.

A friend of yours warns you not to trust your new boss. "He's cold, defensive, and simply doesn't care about his employees. I know—I used to work for him."

Accepting your friend's forewarning, you go forearmed. You keep up your own defenses. You guard your communication.

Your new employer senses your defensiveness and reacts similarly. He doesn't want to be hurt either. Seeing this defensiveness, what do you report to your friend?

"Thanks a lot, friend, I'm glad you told me. He was just like you said."

Now turn the illustration somewhat. This time you're the employer, and a trusted associate confides in you about one of your new employees—"a lazy clock watcher who'll produce only if you hover over him. I know—that's the only way I got anything out of him."

Grateful for the "inside" information, you hover.

However, the employee, with a concept of himself as being dependable and responsible, is eager to demonstrate his self-reliance and resourcefulness in this new job opportunity. His past job was only a means to an end. He wants new and challenging work with satisfactions within itself.

Now put these two attitudes together and watch what happens. "Sure enough," you report to your associate, "just as you said: the man's plain lazy, and hovering supervision's the only hope."

And the employee reports to his wife, "Let's keep looking around. There's no hope in this new job. I can barely wait till four-thirty every day."

These illustrations are typical of scores of daily commonplace occurrences in businesses, in schools, in neighborhoods, in homes. They are self-fulfilling prophecies. (Acting on a belief about the future helps to bring it about, thus self-fulfilling.)

In this very way the ideas and theories we have about leadership, management, parent-child relations, child development, or any subject where the human factor is dominant, tend to prove themselves true. We produce our own evidence. Attitudes create events.

Some, thinking themselves realistic, try to assume nothing; instead, they wait for the "facts" about people, to see what they'll do before making any judgments. These people also lose the tremendous power and motivating influence that is behind, first, clearly expressing belief and trust in others, and then, most important, acting accordingly.

Several studies in both the business world and education strongly point out the powerful influence of the leader's or teacher's attitude on the production and achievement of others. A classic one involved groups of low I.Q.-rated students. Most of the teachers were informed of the low I.Q. scores and taught accordingly. Some were not so informed, assumed normal I.Q. distribution, and treated the students accordingly. The unlabeled students consistently performed better than the labeled ones!

Our efforts to classify and categorize, judge and measure, often emerge from our own insecurities and frustrations in dealing with complex, changing, fluid realities. While our labels may appear neat and realistic and expedient, they may also be damaging, demoralizing, and highly unrealistic.

Each individual person is many things and has many dimensions, many potentials, some in evidence, most still dormant. He's a compound of many facts—even contradictory facts. He tends to react to how we treat him, what we believe about him.

Some may let us down. Some may take advantage of our trust, considering us naive or gullible. But most will come through, many simply because we believed they would. It is best not to bottleneck the many for fear of a few! Whenever we assume good faith, born of good motives and inner security, and then act accordingly, we appeal to whatever good there is in the other, even if there is very little.

The three wise monkeys put it this way: "Hear no evil—see no evil—speak no evil."

Goethe put it another way: "Treat a man as he is and he will remain as he is. Treat a man as he can and should be and he will become as he can and should be."

14

Empathy: A Problem Solver

I'll never forget a teacher friend of mine who was heartsick over his relationship with his teenage son. "When I come into the room where he is reading or watching TV, he gets up and goes out—that's how bad the relationship is," he reported.

I encouraged him to try first to understand his son rather than to try first to get his son to understand him and his advice. He answered, "I already understand him. What he needs is to learn respect for his parents and to show appreciation for all we're trying to do for him."

For the son to really open up, his dad must work on the assumption he doesn't understand his son and perhaps never fully will but that he wants to and will try.

Eventually the father agreed to work on this assumption, for he felt he'd tried about everything else. I assured him he would have to prepare himself for the communication, for it would really test him, particularly his patience and self-control. He'd really have to have his mind made up.

The next evening at about 8:00 P.M. the father approached the son and said, "Son, I'm not happy with our relationship and I'd like to see what we can do to improve it. Perhaps I haven't taken the time to really understand you."

"Boy, I'll say you haven't! You've never understood me!" the son flashed back.

Inside the father burned, and it was about all he could do to keep from retorting, *Why, you ungrateful little whipper snapper! Don't you think I don't understand you! Why, I've gone through the mill. I know the story!*

But he restrained this impulse and said, "Well, son, perhaps I haven't, but I'd like to. Can you help me? For instance, take that blow-up we had last week over the car. Can you tell me how you saw it?"

The son, still angry and smarting inside, gave his defensive explanation. The father again restrained his tendency to rush in with his own self-justifying explanation but decided instead to continue to listen for understanding. He was glad he'd made his mind up to do this before the test came.

As he listened, something marvelous began to happen. His son started to soften. Soon he dropped his defenses and began to open up with some of his real problems and deeper feelings.

The father was so overwhelmed by what was happening between them—for the first time in years—and what he had wanted so badly for so long, he could hardly contain himself. He opened up also and shared some of the deep feelings and concerns as well as understandings he had regarding what had happened in the past. For the first time in years they weren't attacking and defending, but were genuinely trying to understand each other. What happiness it was for both!

Around 10:30 P.M. the mother came in and suggested it was bedtime. The father said they were communicating "for the first time" and wanted to continue.

They visited until after midnight and discussed many things, most of which were far more important to them both than the concerns they had been dueling and fencing around so long. The son had longed for a relationship with his dad, with whom he had identified when he was younger. Inside he had many self-doubts and mixed feelings he wanted to talk about. He would talk to his close friends about some of them but he found himself, in his desire to impress them, never being fully honest. Besides, they listened only in terms of their needs and experiences, so very little real empathy or satisfaction resulted.

The father told me of this experience a few days later and tearfully said, "I feel like I've found my son again and he's found his dad." He was truly grateful he had gone into the experience determined inside to first understand before trying to be understood.

It has always been impressive and instructive that the Prophet Joseph was so struck with the assurance that if he asked God for wisdom he would not be upbraided. Upbraiding means to accuse or reprove.

"I at length came to the determination to 'ask of God,' concluding that if he gave wisdom to them that lacked wisdom, and would give liberally, and not upbraid, I might venture."

Too often we punish honest, open expressions or questions. We upbraid, judge, belittle, embarrass. Others learn to cover up, to protect themselves, to not ask. The greatest single barrier to rich, honest family communication is the tendency to criticize and judge—in short, to upbraid. Watch closely and listen carefully and you'll find this tendency everywhere. Also notice what it does to you.

When we're communicating with another, we need to give full attention, to be "completely present," as one put it. Then we need to empathize—see it from the other's point of view, "walk in his moccasins" for awhile. This takes courage, and patience, and inner sources of security so we're not afraid of new learning or changing what we wanted to say before we began to listen.

15

How to Give an Understanding Response

We've been discussing the power of understanding; now let's practice giving an understanding response. Here's the situation.

For several days you've sensed your fifteen-year-old daughter's unhappiness. You've asked about it but she claimed nothing was wrong, that "everything's okay." One night, while you're doing dishes together, she begins to open up.

"This rule that I can't date until I'm sixteen is embarrassing me to death. I like to follow our leaders' counsel, but all my friends are dating and that's all they can talk about. I feel as if I'm just out of it. Bill keeps asking me out and I keep having to tell him I'm not old enough. I just know he's going to ask me for the big beach party, and if I have to tell him no again, I just know he'll give up on me. So will Carol and Mary. Everyone's talking about it."

How do you respond?

First, think of what your most natural response would be. Would you say, "Oh, don't worry about it, honey, no one's going to give up on you," trying to give assurance? Or would you respond, "Just stick to your guns, Sue. Don't worry so much about what others say and think."

Neither of the above is an understanding response.

The first is an evaluative or judging response in terms of *your* values and *your* needs. The second is advice from *your* point of view or in terms of *your* needs.

Consider two more responses. First, "Tell me what they are saying about you." Second, "When they talk about you they are really secretly admiring you for your stand, and you're just feeling some normal insecurity."

Again, neither response shows that you understand Sue. The first is probing for information *you* feel is important. The second is interpreting what's happening with the friends and inside Sue, as *you* see it.

What would an understanding response be? First, it would attempt to reflect back what Sue feels and says so she would feel you, her mother, understand her feeling and her expression. Example: "You kind of feel torn inside, Sue. You want to follow what our leaders say but you also feel embarrassed when everyone else can date and you have to say no. Is that what you mean?"

She then may respond, "Yes, that's what I mean," and will go on, "but the thing I'm really afraid of is that I won't know how to act around boys when I do start dating. Everyone else is learning and I'm not."

Again, an understanding response would reflect back: "You feel somewhat scared that when the time comes you won't know what to do."

She may say yes and go on further and deeper into her feelings, or she may say, "Well, that's not exactly what I mean. I mean . . ." and she goes on to try to give you a clearer picture of what she's feeling and facing.

By using the understanding response (reflecting back her feeling), three things are beginning to happen.

First, both of you are really getting more understanding, you of her and she of herself. Because you weren't harsh ("Well, I don't care what they say, you know what the rule is!"), because you didn't rush in with judgment or advice or interpretation, thus taking direction of the communication from *your* point of view, she continued to open up into even deeper and more important problems.

Second, from increased understanding and clarity of the problems and feelings come courage and growth in responsible independence.

Sue didn't blame her mother or the leaders or ask for a change in the rule. All she expressed were some of the problems she was facing and her mixed feelings associated with them. If she can express them fully without fear of censure, embarrassment, or ridicule ("and upbraideth not"), she will become inwardly capable and desirous of coping with the situation herself.

Third, through such an effort to understand Sue, her mother is building a real confidence relationship that will prove to be immensely helpful to both over the next several years of schooling, romancing, courting, and marriage, with all the real temptations to stray that the world will provide.

Does all this mean that advice and counsel have no place and that the understanding response is the cure-all? Definitely not. It all depends on the situation and the people involved.

I believe the understanding approach has its greatest value when another person, particularly your husband, wife, or child, wants to talk about a problem or some feelings, when a lot of emotion is involved. If you seek to understand until the other feels understood and so states, it might then be most appropriate, based on your discernment, to give counsel, even strong counsel. Feeling understood and accepted, the other person will receive and respect your counsel better than before.

Test the value of an understanding response for yourself in three ways: (1) practice empathy when listening to another; (2) practice refraining from advising, judging, sympathizing, or interpreting; (3) practice reflecting or mirroring back the content, and particularly the feeling, of the other's expression.

In your practicing you will learn many things about others and about yourself.

One last word: the understanding response is more an attitude than a technique. It will fail if you're just trying to

16

If Offended, Take the Initiative

At the end of a speech on the importance of "going to the one who offended you," an individual approached me and said, "I liked your speech enough to do what you said. You offended me once and, frankly, I've discounted all you've said since."

He said that he was attending a fireside speech and had to leave for a minute in the middle. "As I walked down the aisle you commented, 'Don't run away mad,' and everybody laughed. I was embarrassed to leave as it was, but that comment, and everyone's laugh, knifed right into me. When I returned I sat in the back, still smarting and angry inside. I was so upset I could hardly listen to what you said then, and I felt about the same way even tonight."

This individual took the initiative to come to me rather than nursing his hurt and judging privately, thus fortifying the barrier between us. We both learned and benefited from the experience.

"And if thy brother or sister offend thee, thou shalt take him or her between him or her and thee alone; and if he or she confess thou shalt be reconciled." (D&C 42:88.)

Why is the initiative with the one who has been offended, when the natural tendency when we are offended is to say within ourselves, "He is the one at fault; therefore he should come to me."

Oftentimes a person offends unknowingly, as I had in the above situation. If someone offends you unknowingly and continues to do so, you are responsible for the strain in the relationship if you do not take the initiative to clear it up. Often you'll find you made unrealistic expectations. You may discover you simply didn't understand the situation at all.

One lady told me that for a long time she felt that her own husband had been unjustly treated by a leader in her stake. The resentment grew and grew until her children were similarly inflicted by this poisonous venom and the attitude of the entire family toward this man, his family, his business, and his stake leadership became critical and negative.

Eventually she took the initiative to go to him, and she returned with feelings of gratitude and sorrow—gratitude for clearing it up and sorrow because she learned the other side of the story. She had not acted on the entire picture. She was sick to think how long she had mothered such hostile feelings on the basis of a completely inaccurate understanding.

Consider two tragic consequences of not taking the initiative. First, the one offended often broods about the offense until the situation is blown all out of proportion. Like a poison, bitterness and resentment spread and afflict other relationships and situations totally removed from the initial one. Then guilt grows within, causing anger to flash and bite, feeding on the weaknesses of others. Eventually the mounting vindictive spirit can contain itself no longer, and it explodes irrationally at the slightest provocation on its "enemy," inflicting wounds and scars that may never be healed. Now the whole problem has changed, both in location and in complexity. The offended becomes the offender.

Second, sometimes we make expectations of another, and when he doesn't come through, we are offended. We then judge and behave defensively to avoid further hurt. The other sees this defensiveness and may react similarly, thus giving us new evidence to support our earlier judgments. We, the offended, bring about the very treatment we feared. This is the self-fulfilling prophecy.

Obviously, therefore, it's better not to take offense, whether intended or not. It's best not to judge another at all but to forgive "seven times seventy," if need be.

But if we are offended and we can't fully forgive or resolve it inside, we should go to the other shortly after the offense so reconciliation can take place.

I give two suggestions in taking the initiative.

First, we should do this in a good spirit, in control, not in the spirit of vindication and anger, to avoid giving offense ourself, thus compounding the problem. The roots of the courage to admit we were offended are spiritual.

Second, we should describe our feelings—when the offense took place—rather than judge or label the other. To say "I felt belittled and so embarrassed" is more accurate and less offensive than to say "your dominating attitude" or "your childish behavior." This preserves the dignity and self-respect of the other, who then can respond and learn without feeling threatened.

We must be aware that our feelings, opinions, and perceptions are not facts. To act on that awareness takes thought control and fosters humility.

17

Paying the Uttermost Farthing

"My biggest worry and concern is my poor relationship with my fourteen-year-old son. I have set a poor example in the past with my yelling and losing my temper. How can I erase this image he has of me?" a father asked.

Perhaps there is no greater heartbreak than for parents to feel they are losing or have lost contact and influence with a son or daughter who is being drawn more and more into the lower roads of life.

What can be done in such a tragic situation? Fortunately a great deal can be done. Few, if any, situations are hopeless. There are yet several approaches, including the prayer of faith, which can be taken to heal the broken relationship and to exercise righteous influence again.

One of these approaches is to pay "the uttermost farthing." Consider very carefully a possible meaning of a teaching in the Savior's Sermon on the Mount:

"Agree with thine adversary quickly, whiles thou art in the way with him; lest at any time the adversary deliver thee to the judge, and the judge deliver thee to the officer, and thou be cast into prison.

"Verily I say unto thee, Thou shalt by no means come out thence, till thou has paid the uttermost farthing." (Matt 5:25-26.)

Applying this teaching to any seriously broken or

strained relationship—not just the family—I emphasize six points.

1. We may honestly admit to ourselves, as the father above did, that we are at least partly to blame for the problem. Reflecting back, we can remember how we might have embarrassed, insulted, or belittled, or how we simply didn't take the time to understand, or how we were inconsistent in discipline or conditional in love. We may have felt justified at the time but now we realize that we simply lost control and gratified our pride. In short, we were unfair. We hurt another.

2. When one is deeply hurt or embarrassed, he draws back and closes up. One of the safest ways to avoid future hurt from us is to simply distrust us. In this sense we have been judged as unkind, unfair, or not understanding, and put behind prison bars and walls in his own mind. Expecting nothing, he can then never be disappointed. He simply refuses to believe, to open up, to "release" us from the image or mental prison he has us in.

3. Improving our behavior alone won't release us from this prison, simply because he can't afford to trust us again. It's too risky. He's suspicious of this new behavior, this new kind face, this "insincere" entreaty. "I trusted him before and look what happened."

Although inside he is crying out for parental direction and emotional support—playing roles and pretending adequacy is fatiguing—still we remain "judged" in his mental prison for an indeterminate sentence.

4. Often the only way out is to go to him and admit our mistakes, apologize, and ask forgiveness. In this reconciliation we must become very, very specific in describing exactly what we did that was wrong. We must make no excuses or apologies, explanations or defenses. But let it clearly stand that we know we did wrong and that we are sincerely sorry. Then, in his own mind—where we are in prison—he knows we understand exactly what put us there and are paying the specific price of release.

Sometimes we make a stab at this process but inwardly

hold back, saying to ourself, "He should be sorry also. I can only go so far but no further until he acknowledges his part and seeks forgiveness also." This kind of peacemaking is superficial, insincere, and manipulative. While it might temporarily calm the waters on the surface, the suspicious turbulence underneath still rages and the next stress situation on the relationship will reveal it. The "uttermost farthing" means exactly that. The uttermost—not the first, second, or third, but the uttermost.

5. This approach must be utterly sincere and not used as a manipulative technique to bring the other around.

If this approach is used only because it works, it will boomerang, for unless a real and sincere change takes place deep within us, sooner or later we'll trespass again on tender feelings and the new mental prison will have thicker walls than ever. He simply will not believe us when we say again how sorry we are. Repeated token repentance wins no confidence, human or divine.

6. I believe this approach will work in most situations, in time, both in obtaining a release from "prison," with its new opportunity to communicate and to influence, and in inspiring, not forcing, the other to make some hard admissions and resolves also.

18

Let Quarrels Fly Out Open Windows

On December 1, 1969, a great storm, centered around the Aleutian Islands, spawned and drove huge waves toward the island chain of Hawaii, almost two thousand miles away. The surf built and built until some of the highest waves (50 to 60 feet) ever reported in Oahu's recent past began to pound her north shore.

It seemed so ironical: beautiful clear days, almost idyllic; yet the presence of this snarling, snapping, white-fanged sea monster.

The irony invited thousands of natives and tourists to come and see. But how deceiving! We thought we were in a good safe position, standing with everybody else many feet from the high-water mark of past waves, and then out on the horizon we could see an unusually large one rolling in. Everyone commented curiously at first, but as it came closer the danger became apparent and we ran. Twice that afternoon, hundreds of us watching from the so-called secure high shelf were enveloped in water to our knees.

Those who lived there were enveloped by terror. One couple watched in horror as a wave pushed their two-year-old girl, crib and all, out into the yard, where a wall then collapsed on her.

Many were literally sucked out of their cars; others were dragged off streets and out of service stations. A few were killed, many were injured, many were rescued. Scores of shore homes were blown apart; hundreds were damaged.

Days after the surf serpent had spent her fury we visited the destruction. I'll never forget seeing two homes, side by side, high up on Sunset Beach. One solidly built on a cement foundation was of good brick construction. The other was flimsy and frame, but standing three feet high on stilts.

When the waves reached the solid front wall of the first home, they had no place to go but through it. It literally exploded; all that was left was the good solid foundation and part of the side walls.

But when the waves slammed against the flimsy neighbor, they had somewhere to go—under it! It "withstood the rude blast" with almost no damage.

This whole experience reminded me of the German expression, "Let arguments fly out open windows." As I understand it, this means to give no answer to a contentious argument or an irresponsible accusation. Let such "fly out open windows" until they spend themselves. If you try to answer or reason back, you only serve to gratify and ignite the pent-up hostility and anger within, just as the solid wall ignited the pent-up power of the wave that destroyed it.

Your reasoning in such an argument may be sound, your logic consistent and convincing—but it isn't a matter of reason and logic. The battlefield is emotion, sometimes unbridled explosive emotion, and sometimes raw feeling veiled by a thin veneer of seeming reasonableness and sincerity.

As with the north shore that beautiful day, it may also seem at first a pleasant sunny situation, but the real source of the interpersonal storm that seems to erupt at the slightest provocation has its source in other places, in other problems, generally personal, and may have been building for days, months, even years.

When you remain silent, giving no answer, and go quietly about your business, the other has to struggle with the natural consequences of irresponsible expression. He or she may grow reasonable and may even apologize for taking it out on you or for being so irresponsible and childish. Sometimes merely restating or mirroring back the other's hostile comments will reveal to him his irresponsibility. But an answer only justifies the irresponsible spirit, and the argument reduces itself to an ego battle, however well masked by clever language. And no one ever wins one of these.

We must not allow ourselves to be drawn, either through our curiosity or our defensiveness, into any poisonous, contentious orbit or we will find ourselves bitten and afflicted similarly. Then others' weaknesses will become our own, and all this will sow a seedbed of future misunderstandings, accusations, and wranglings.

It is highly significant that the very first message the Savior delivered to the Nephites contained strong counsel against both doctrinal disputations and the spirit of contention.

"For verily, verily I say unto you, he that hath the spirit of contention is not of me, but is of the devil, who is the father of contention, and he stirreth up the hearts of men to contend with anger, one with another.

"Behold, this is not my doctrine, to stir up the hearts of men with anger, one against another; but this is my doctrine, that such things should be done away." (3 Nephi 11:29-30.)

The power to be still, to be patient, and to let arguments fly out open windows comes partially from understanding this very principle, but primarily it flows out of an inward peace and unity that is freed of the compulsive need to answer and justify. And the source of this peace is living responsibly, in control, and obedient to conscience.

III

FAMILY

19

Build Harmony in Your Family

The late secretary-general of the United Nations, Dag Hammarskjold, once made this profound observation: "It is more noble to give yourself completely to one individual than to labor diligently for the salvation of the masses."

A father could be terribly involved and dedicated to his work, to church and community projects, and to many people's lives, yet not have a deep, meaningful relationship with his own wife. It would certainly take more nobility of character, more humility, more patience and understanding for him to develop such a relationship with one person, his wife, than it would take to give continued dedicated service to the many.

A bishop, a priesthood leader, or an auxiliary executive can be ever so devoted to working for the salvation of others, but perhaps be unwilling to do that which is necessary to build a rich relationship and meaningful two-way communication with a teenage son or daughter. To the many he serves by giving his time and talents, but to the one he may need to give more of himself, perhaps even his pride.

Some may even justify neglecting the one to take care of the many, feeling sustained in this attitude by many expressions of esteem and gratitude. Yet in quiet moments, within, we know differently. "No other success can compensate for failure in the home." (David O. McKay.)

The Savior again is our standard, our model. He spent most of his ministry with a few individuals. Many of his most significant messages and teachings were given to or about one or two individuals. The real, deep conversion of these few disciples has changed the history of the world for all the rest of us.

One Saturday morning the phone interrupted some quiet office work. It was my wife asking me if I couldn't come home and give some help. "I've got an appointment downtown in less than thirty minutes; I've still got to bathe the babies, and the other kids just aren't doing their work this morning. (Background noises punctuated this point.) Besides, I haven't even changed my clothes yet."

I explained I was preparing for a meeting and couldn't come but would give some advice. (Advice from quiet sidelines to those fighting it out in the arena is always easy and often cheap.)

I knew if my wife could get willing cooperation from our oldest daughter her problem would be solved. "But she won't cooperate at all this morning," she replied.

"Take her into her bedroom alone for just a few minutes and give yourself to her. Listen to see what's bothering her," I suggested.

"I haven't time to do that."

Then I quoted something that has come to have meaning to both of us. "Too busy sawing to take time to sharpen the saw?"

"Okay, I'll try."

Our daughter knew what was happening, and as soon as she felt she was being sincerely listened to and valued, she immediately told her mother, "Just get changed. I'll take care of the kids and clean up."

The depth and quality of the unity between a husband and wife, between a priesthood leader and his counselors, between an employer and his immediate staff, between a parent and a child, is being communicated—radiated—constantly.

We need to set aside uninterrupted blocks of time in

giving ourselves completely to one, in being "completely present."

Harmony cannot be feigned or pretended. Others will sense it and their confidence in our sincerity and integrity will be strengthened or weakened, as the case might be. Nothing undermines confidence (often unjustifiably) in a leader or a teacher quite as much as the feeling that he can't even govern himself (or his household or immediate staff) by the principles he teaches. Such a feeling diffuses itself throughout the entire organization and punctures the spirit of devoted service.

And nothing builds confidence in another's leadership and teachings quite as much as the example of harmony, mutual consideration, and selfless devotion that that person has with the key people of his life. Such a person doesn't have to testify of himself. Others do it—his works do it.

20

Talking Through Differences

If we are careful observers, we can see our own weaknesses reappear in the lives of our children. Perhaps in nothing is this so evident as in the way differences and disagreements are handled.

To illustrate, a mother goes to the family room to call her sons to lunch and finds them arguing and fighting over a toy. "Boys, I've told you before not to fight! You work it out so each has a turn." The older grabs it away from his smaller brother with "I'm first!" The younger cries and refuses to come to lunch.

The mother, puzzled by why her boys never seem to learn, reflects for a moment on her own handling of differences with her husband. She remembers "only last night" when they had a sharp exchange over a matter of finances. She remembers "only this morning" when her husband summarily left for work without the best of feelings after a disagreement on plans for the evening.

In fact, the more this mother reflects, the more apparent it becomes that she and her husband have in reality demonstrated over and over again how *not* to handle differences and disagreements. They have taught their children, by example, to either fight or flight whenever they disagree.

Fighting takes many forms, ranging from violence

and open expressions of anger and hate to subtle sarcasm, sharp answers, clever comebacks, belittling humor, and various kinds of cold, sophisticated judging and rejecting. Usually, out of guilt, the fighter also releases much of the stored-up venom and bitterness on himself. Guilt and anger are generally two sides of the same coin.

Flighting ("copping out," escaping) also takes various forms. The most common is to simply withdraw, feeling bad toward the other and sorry for oneself. Such sulking often feeds the fires of revenge and future retaliation.

People also flee by growing cold and indifferent, by escaping involvement and responsibility in their own world into the fabricated worlds of TV and movies or the unreal world of drugs and drink or the alluring world of illicit romance.

Because each person in a family is different and unique, differences are inevitable. Furthermore, for purposes of balance and growth, they are necessary, even desirable. Latent upbringing and temperamental differences will surface under pressures and stresses, with changing circumstances and expanding responsibilities.

When such differences arise, parents have a supreme teaching opportunity. They can show a new way of coping with them—a third alternative.

They can teach their plastic, highly impressionable children, by example, how to talk through differences and disagreements, even how to "agree to disagree agreeably."

Two intertwined elements are foundational in this third alternative, this talking-through approach.

First, both parents have and continually renew their basic commitment to the things that unite them. Their deepest loyalties and strongest feelings attach to these fundamental things rather than to the problems or issues around which differences may emerge. Differences are not ignored; they are subordinated. The issue or one's point is never as important as the relationship.

Second, the parents show respect for each other by the way they listen to and address each other, by the kindness and gentleness in their tone of voice, by their willingness to give and take, and by their coming finally to an agreement that they unitedly sustain.

The first two alternatives—fighting and flighting—represent the immature course of least resistance and involve no internal control and discipline. Sometimes, in the heat of the moment, we may need to temporarily withdraw for perspective and control. But self-restraint, respect, and love for the other and the courage to face realities are the heart and fabric of the talking-through approach.

As in the Savior's parables, such responsible peace-making, so greatly needed in a day of violence and noninvolvement, naturally follows and is empowered by a pure heart.

21

The Importance of Timing in Teaching

There's a time to teach and a time not to teach.

The father in the following illustration was unaware of the latter. Perhaps his approach isn't too different from those used by many of the rest of us.

Returning home from work late one afternoon, he stepped into quite a scene. There, in the corner, was his little birthday girl, Sue, defiantly grasping all of her presents, unwilling to let other eager hands play with them.

All eyes were on Sue, and to the father it appeared that everyone was disappointed with this selfish display by his own daughter. He particularly felt the expectations of several parents who had come to pick up their children.

The father knew he should teach his daughter to share, so he moved in to teach sharing. He used five methods.

First, a simple request. "Honey, it would be nice to share your presents with your friends for a few minutes before they go home."

"No! I don't want to." Her ego was invested in her refusal.

Second, a little reasoning. "Honey, if you learn to share your toys with them when they are at your home, then when you go to their homes they will share their toys with you."

Again, "No!"

The daddy, feeling more social breath on his neck, was beginning to invest his ego also in his teaching effort.

Third, bribery. Very softly, "Sue, if you'll share I'll give you a piece of gum."

"I don't care. I don't want a piece of gum!" she exploded.

Fourth, fear and threat. In exasperation, "Unless you share, Sue, you'll be in trouble. I mean, after all, they gave you these things."

"I don't care. These are my things. I don't have to share."

Last method, force. The father merely took away some of the toys and gave them to the other kids. "Here, kids, play with them."

How foolish this father was. He couldn't give understanding so he expected his little girl to give things. Because he feared social disapproval more than he valued Sue's growth, he couldn't give respect for Sue's right to possess before she chose on her own to share.

In his effort to teach sharing, he exemplified selfishness.

A wise father could have sensed what was happening and, after a simple request or two, understood and honored Sue's right to possess the things she had just been given. He then might have directed the attention off Sue and onto an interesting game or activity. This is teaching by example.

Then, at a later time, when the feeling was good, he could teach the value of sharing by precept (telling, explaining). Sue would share—naturally, freely—out of her own desire.

Consider four suggestions on *when* to teach.

1. Discern the over-all situation. If people are "in threat," an effort to teach by precept will generally increase the resentment both toward the teacher and his teaching.

It's often better to wait for or to create a new situation in which the person is in a secure and receptive frame of mind. Your very forbearance in not scolding or correcting in the emotionally charged moment will communicate and teach respect and understanding.

In other words, when you can't teach one value by precept, you can teach one by example. And example teaching is infinitely more powerful and lasting than precept teaching. Combining both, of course, is even better.

2. Sense your own spirit and attitude. If you're angry and frustrated, you can't avoid communicating this regardless of the logic of your words or the value of the principle you're trying to teach.

Restrain yourself. Or go apart. Then teach another time, when you have feelings of affection, respect, and inward security.

A good rule of thumb: If you can hold the arm or hand of your son or daughter while correcting or teaching and you both feel comfortable in this, you'll have a positive influence. You simply can't do this in an angry mood.

3. Distinguish between the time to teach and the time to give help and support. To rush in with preachments and success formulas when your spouse or child is emotionally low or fatigued or under a lot of pressure is comparable to trying to teach a drowning man to swim. He needs a rope or a helping hand, not a lecture.

4. Realize that in a larger sense, we are teaching one thing or another all of the time, because we are constantly radiating what we are.

22

Unity and Consistency in Discipline

At ten o'clock one night, returning home from the office, I was sitting alone in my study going over some mail when my four-year-old son suddenly appeared at the door. I looked up, surprised. He just stood there expressionless. I'd had a good day and felt good inside and was so happy to see my boy. "Hi, Michael Sean! How are you?"

He said nothing, just whipped around, ran to the top of the stairs, and yelled down, "Hey, Stephen! He's nice!"

In other words he said, "Daddy's in a good mood tonight. It's safe to come up and play. He'll protect us from Mommy."

Mommy had put them down long before—several times! The last time they knew she meant it. But when they heard Daddy's car drive up, new hope was born again.

With fresh courage Stephen, the older, wiser son, had sent his naive brother up to "test the wind."

Sure enough, the wind was fair, and before long Daddy was trying to explain things to Mommy. Another victory, however short.

This homely incident is an illustration of some vital principles of discipline in the home. Rules and limits and consequences must be (1) clearly established, (2) agreed upon by both parents, (3) understood by the children, and (4) consistently followed through on.

When discipline is based on the mood of the moment, no one knows what is expected or what will happen. Personal security is largely born of a sense of justice—knowing what is expected, what the limits and rules are, and what the consequences are of honoring or dishonoring them.

We all know how we would react if, in the middle of chess, our opponent were to suddenly begin to move his castle like a queen, explaining he'd changed the rules "in order to even things up."

Similarly, the whole game of life can be thrown out of kilter with uncertain expectations and shifting of limits or arbitrary rule making. One day this, the next day that. One day, permissive indulgence; the next, unfair control.

The impact of this on a child's, or anyone's, personal security can be disastrous. In one sense a person's security comes from being able to answer the question, "What can I depend on?" Think about it. "What can I depend on?"

I'm convinced that for a young person to be able to answer that question is far more important than for parents to answer the question, "What method of discipline is best?"

I further believe that children's concepts of God and their feelings toward him and toward his rules and his limits and his consequences are initially and largely formed out of the justice and security they experience in the home. I extend this reasoning to include any form of human authority

No wonder many grow up learning to depend only on their own ability to manipulate people and life. They learn how to just about talk themselves into or out of almost any situation. Since the rules of life for them shift and can be influenced, why not learn how? "Is there any security in any other way?" they reason.

One of the most effective ways is to pit one parent against the other—learn how to test the wind—cater to the most lenient—get him to carry your banner and fight. Children learn early how to get parents to argue with each other over the matter. "Keep the heat off us—one way or another we can get out of the consequences," they say.

When life becomes a game to be manipulated, its sin becomes getting caught. A distorted social conscience eclipses the divine conscience. The way back then is very hard, for so much has to be unlearned first.

I see three lessons in this story and analysis for all of us as parents, teachers, or leaders.

First, we (husband and wife) need to achieve a deep harmony and agreement on what the limits and rules and expectations are and to be deeply committed to following through with the agreed-upon consequences.

Second, these decisions should be clearly communicated and understood by our children. Genuinely involving them in setting rules and consequences is desirable to the extent that they evidence the maturity in judgment and responsibleness in action.

Third (and perhaps this should be first), to do these two things assumes a great deal about the quality of our own personal lives and of our relationship with each other and with them. We must live what we teach.

It's obviously impossible to communicate clearly and to discipline consistently when our own lives are undisciplined and inconsistent. And how long can we pretend harmony on these crucial matters with our mates when such harmony doesn't exist? The first real incident will expose us!

We inevitably return to the spiritual roots of our lives.

23

Don't Give Up and Don't Give In

What can we do to stop misbehavior? What can we do to establish patterns of right behavior? Perhaps these two questions are either thought about or asked more often by parents, teachers, and leaders than any other two. The answers are obviously not simple. So much depends on the situation and the people involved.

One approach is highly effective in many situations: reality therapy.

A few years ago a young psychiatrist, Dr. William Glasser, developed this approach initially for the professional handling of mentally and emotionally disturbed people, working on a radically different and untraditional theory.

Basically, the theory is: man's basic psychological needs are to love and be loved and to feel worthwhile to himself and to others, and the only way to satisfy and fulfill these needs is to behave responsibly and do what is right. In short, to feel better, we must behave better.

Building on this theory, the approach could be as follows:

1. Become personally involved with the misbehaving person so as to show that you genuinely care about him, that you regard him as a person of worth, that you won't give up on him.

2. Focus on *what* he is *doing* in the present, not on *why* he's doing it, on what he is feeling, or on his past.

When a person excuses his misbehavior by blaming others or circumstances or feelings, he feels less responsible for it. Then he logically reasons within himself, "Since I'm not responsible, I'm not expected to and I can't behave responsibly."

Therefore no excuses for misbehavior can be accepted. While we are not responsible for all that happens to us, we are responsible for how we react.

3. Then ask the person, "What happens when you behave this way?" and "Is that what you want?" In this way you are bringing reality into the situation. He must face it and must judge whether he likes the consequences or not.

4. Finally, ask: "What did you want to do about it?" and when appropriate, "Is there any way I can help?" Here the person makes his own decision or plan and you show care by offering help.

Now, to illustrate, consider the following abbreviated dialogue.

Mother: "What are you doing, son?"

Son: "Watching a movie on TV." (He identifies his own behavior.)

Mother: "Earlier you said you needed several hours to prepare for your midterm tests tomorrow. How do you expect to do on them?"

Son: "Good, I hope. I'll study after the movie. It's so interesting."

Mother: "What happened last time you studied half the night for your tests?"

Son: "I really messed up." (He identifies possible consequences.)

Mother: "Is that what you want this time?"

Son: "No, I don't." (He judges.)

Mother: "What should you do?"

Son: "I had better get at it now." (He decides.)

Mother: "Fine. I'll try to keep the kids quiet while you study."

Reality therapy is sometimes seen and experienced as a harsh, cold, unfeeling technique of facing the misbehaving person up to the realities of life.

Yet the most powerful and the most difficult aspect behind reality therapy is the personal warmth and emotional involvement of the one practicing it. It takes little courage to be strong and firm with people we don't really care for. It's caring that brings our courage into play.

It is also unkind to shield people from the consequences of their own behavior. In doing so we teach them they are inadequate and weak. Further, when we give in to irresponsible behavior—by excusing it or sympathizing with it—we condone and actually foster spoiled, law-unto-self behavior. But, if we give up—by ignoring them or tearing into them—we undermine their motivation to try.

Dr. Glasser wrote: "Parents who are willing to suffer the pain of the child's intense anger by firmly holding him to the responsible course are teaching him a lesson that will help him all his life."

This kind of discipline, tempered with love, can only come from responsible, disciplined lives. Otherwise, we will take the course of least resistance—giving in when we care or giving up when we don't.

The story is told of a boy who was spellbound in watching the metamorphosis of a butterfly out of its cocoon. One last tendon kept the butterfly bound. It struggled, thrashed about, and fought to break free. No success. The boy's sympathies led him to cut that remaining thin tendon with his pen knife. At last the butterfly was free! But it never flew. Undeveloped muscles.

24

How Attitudes Create Events

H_2O. What is it? We normally think of it as the chemical formula for water. What states does it exist in? Liquid, gas, and solid. What is its natural state? We can't say. That depends on the pressure and the temperature in the situation.

So also with people. To a considerable extent we are all like H_2O. We are in a constant state of radiation and absorption—radiating our feelings and attitudes, absorbing the feelings and attitudes of others. Our own attitude, our state of mind, as it were, is largely a function of the attitudes of those around us. Similarly the attitudes of those we live and work around are largely a function of our own attitude. The implication of that last sentence is profound and far reaching.

As parents, teachers, and leaders we can use this knowledge to influence, even determine, the attitudes of others and therefore the main circumstances of our lives.

This H_2O thinking is particularly applicable in our homes, with our loved ones, for at least two reasons.

First, because our lives are so emotionally interwoven with each other. We depend heavily on home and family for emotional release and for emotional support, for nurturing hopes and plans, for nursing wounds.

Second, because in the social safety and comfort of

home we drop our roles. We let down. We become our-selves. And often, particularly when we are tired or low, we become our worst selves. We take advantage. We take each other for granted. We forget small courtesies. We for-get to say "please" and "thank you" and "I'm sorry" and "what is your feeling?" We get too full of ourselves, of our own needs, to accurately sense and appropriately respond to the needs of others or of situations.

Sometimes we even release our pent-up frustrations and anger on the innocent, on those near and dear to us. And, because their emotional needs are so tied to our atti-tudes, they are hurt at first, and they withdraw. Sometimes, however, to protect themselves against further hurts, they respond in kind. They also wrongly learn that the best defense is a good offense.

In this way many good marriages deteriorate. Criti-cism, nagging, sharp exchanges, belittling humor, sarcasm, and cynicism pollute the emotional climate of the home. And the children grow up touchy, angry, fearful, and in-secure.

President and Sister David O. McKay were magnifi-cent models of sincerity and consistency in living lives of mutual respect and consideration. Sister McKay once re-marked, "My husband treats me the same in private as he does in public."

Perhaps it is because our home is our greatest respon-sibility that it is also our greatest leadership challenge and character test. It is a test of whether we practice in private what we preach in public, a test of our integrity in living by a single standard.

In public, social expectations define roles for us. These expectations put brakes on our tongue and restraints on our behavior.

Is this true with you? To find out, ask yourself how you would handle a difference on an emotionally charged issue with your spouse or child if a house guest were in the background, and then how you would handle it if one were not there. Further, ask yourself how you would discipline an unruly child in each situation.

Speaking for myself, I remember talking to my wife somewhat critically over the phone once about something that had upset me. Suddenly I became aware of the presence of someone in the next office. What a break on my tongue! How i changed my tone of voice! What hypocrisy I felt.

In our long-term struggle for true maturity and integrity, consider one simple but amazingly helpful practice.

Mother, before the children return from school full of their own needs, and before your husband returns from work (or whatever the crossroad situation is), stop and pause. Get control. Plumb your resources. Set your mind and heart. Choose pleasantness and cheerfulness. Choose to give full attention, to supply needs.

Father, sit an extra moment in the car before coming in and do the same. Ask yourself, "How can I bless my wife and children tonight?" Plumb your resources. Choosing to be your best self will arrest fatigue and renew your spirit.

Then watch H_2O—how attitudes create events.

25

Helping Youth at the Crossroads

One of our gravest concerns is the tendency of our youth to make decisions that have important long-range consequences on the basis of short-range emotional perspectives.

We have seen young people go steady because "everyone else is doing it." We've even seen young people go into early engagements and early marriages far before they are prepared for the inevitable tests and responsibilities, in the name of love alone—or again out of a sense of personal insecurity or home frustration.

We have seen young people drop out of school in order to make car payments. I've personally seen college students at the end of a most exasperating registration process select courses, and even majors, on the basis of the shortest line!

We have seen young people turn down mission calls or a temple marriage out of fear of what others may think, or go into the mission field or into a temple marriage without any real understanding and commitment because of social pressure.

Why? Why this tendency to make important crossroad decisions—involving education, marriage, careers, etc.—on the basis of strong emotions and moods?

I'm sure there are many reasons, but I suggest the threads of personal insecurity and self-doubt run through most of them. And, of course, the roots of these feelings and fears lie deep in the history of each person, his upbringing, home life, and choices.

But what do we as parents, teachers, and leaders do now, with the situation as it is? This is the practical question.

Often we won't face this practical here-and-now question. In our justifiable desire to right the wrong, we rush in with judgments, with "shoulds" and "should nots." In a sense we try to change or retrieve the irretrievable past through words.

"You should not think that way." "School is much more important than a car." "You're too young to get married—you don't know what it involves." "You really 'oughta wanna' go on a mission."

What happens? Often to their ears this well-meaning and well-founded advice comes across as: "Don't be that way. Don't think that way. Don't feel that way. Don't be you. *I* just can't stand it if *you're* like that."

Then, out of a renewed desperate clinging for identity and worth, they often rebel and seek their unworthy ends more aggressively and defensively than ever.

In return we moralize and react more justifiably, and more ineffectively, than ever.

Somehow we need to break and reverse this destructive, overreactive, self-feeding cycle. For unless we do it, who will influence our children's crossroad decisions? Their friends will. But their friends are young too, with similar tendencies. Generally they advise from extremely limited perspectives and experiences and usually out of their own needs, without stewardship and inspiration.

Consider two suggestions in meeting this difficult challenge.

First, think before you react. Don't be controlled by your own short-range emotional moods and do something that injures whatever relationship and influence you now have. Unless you are in control and act from within out of deeply anchored, true principles, you won't be able to apply the next suggestion.

Second, try to understand that people tend to act in terms of how they feel instead of what they know. Motivation is more a function of the heart than the head. It isn't what a person thinks he should do, but rather how he feels about that *should* and about himself that motivates him.

When we sense that our language of reason and logic isn't communicating with their language of sentiment and emotion, we should try to understand their language as we would a foreign tongue, without condemning it or rejecting them. We should try to empathize, to reach out to understand how the other sees it and feels it. This very effort communicates respect and acceptance. Defenses lower. The need to fight diminishes. The desire to do what is right is generally set back into motion.

Because a young person's unique problem, feelings, and worth first influence us to understand rather than to judge, then our encouragement and counsel to make long-range decisions on long-range or eternal perspectives will influence him. Influence is a two-way street.

26

Speak Two Languages: Logic and Feeling

I'll never forget my first real encounter with the language barrier. It took place in the streets of Paris on Bastille Day, July 12, 1952, when I was still single.

Perhaps out of the sole desire to be able to say that I had danced in the streets of Paris, I invited a lovely young French girl to dance. She first looked to her guardian uncle for permission and then nodded her assent to me.

What a lost, insecure, frustrating feeling! We were totally unable to communicate with each other. (Remember, this was in the days when it was customary to visit while dancing.) We talked, trying to communicate, but in vain. We simply knew nothing of each other's language. Our only communication was in a common understanding of our plight, with its strain of embarrassed laughter.

I often remember that experience and those feelings whenever I find myself in a difficult communication situation. And it helps, because it makes me realize, in at least two ways, the tremendous effort that genuine and successful communication involves.

First, the language of logic and the language of feeling are as different, in the fundamental sense, as English and French. But the problem is we often don't realize this. The mother thinks she can successfully tell her children to cooperate when they are crying out "unfair! unfair!" The husband thinks he can logically point out where his wife needs to improve after her all-day fatiguing battle with the kids. The leader thinks he can successfully explain why Sue should not marry Tom until he joins the Church, while Sue feels that "you don't understand; with us it's different. I love him so and he loves me."

Thinking we understand, we tell instead of ask. Feeling little need for feedback, we talk instead of listen.

Second, when we realize we don't have a common language, we really reach out to each other. We learn to communicate in other ways. We search and seek for understanding of another, for a sense or spirit of what he or she means, without judging or rejecting or making one an offender for a word.

We need to use our "big communication guns" more in our counseling and relating—that is, to communicate our basic feelings, often before or at least alongside our logical explanations.

How is this done? Consider four ways and note how each is a form of emotional communication that helps eradicate the causes of many communication breakdowns—self-doubt and judgment.

1. Give time. Time is our scarcest resource, and therefore our most valuable one. Our children and others constantly see how we value time, how the clock and deadlines manage our lives. They also often see and feel how interruptions of it are punished.

We may think, in our hurry-hurry world, that we are accomplishing nothing when we just spend time with or by another person. The opposite is often the case, for when we cheerfully give time, we are transferring its worth to another, together with all the values embodied in our example and character.

One rich private visit or a date with one child—focused on that child's interests—will work wonders in righteous motivation.

2. Be patient. Patience (long-suffering) also communicates worth to another, for it says, "I'll go at your

speed. I'm happy to wait for you. You're worth it." Authority's greatest influence often stems from purposely refraining from its use in favor of persuasion, kindness, and patience.

3. Seek to understand. Many people spend much of their energy fighting and struggling for acceptance and identity, for understanding and respect. An honest effort to understand eliminates this need to fight and to defend. In fact, the effort alone, successful or not, communicates acceptance and respect for the essential human worth and dignity of another.

Feelings, not logic, do this.

4. Openly express feelings. Words that are backed up by and congruent with tone of voice, facial expressions, sacrifices, and other nonverbal works are magnified many times in their power to influence, uplift, and bless.

Fundamentally, it takes a lot of self-honesty, self-mastery, and purity to be able to effectively speak the languages of both logic and feeling.

27

Have Frequent Private Visits

Years ago, the daughter of a mission president asked her father what he was doing when he visited privately with each missionary. "I'm holding interviews to help the missionaries with their problems," he answered.

"Daddy, why can't I have an interview? I hardly ever get to discuss my problems alone with you."

To that young daughter the word *interview* meant a time to be alone with her father discussing whatever she wanted to. Her interests, her problems, her concerns were to control the interaction, rather than his. This was the basic ground rule.

The father accepted her definition and started a practice of holding private interviews with each child on a weekly or biweekly basis. It continues to this day. In fact, it is not uncommon at any time for one of his children to say, "Daddy, I want an interview."

Consider two significant benefits of such a practice.

First, each child knows he will have his day in court, an unrushed time when the full attention of the parent is given to his problems and concerns. Relatively few young people (or adults, for that matter) have the experience of being fully listened to without fear of being censored, lectured, or compared.

To simply know one can have an understanding private talk in the future inspires responsible behavior in the present. The frustrating feeling that no one will really listen, much less understand, leads to irresponsible behavior, even to extreme irrational measures calculated to get attention at any cost.

Second, from the unguarded private visit will flow increased warmth, affection, understanding, and confidence. Parents will be both startled and enlightened by the openness and by the live concerns and interests of their youth. And the youth will, in turn, vividly sense the sincerity and depth of concern and interest in their parents and will therefore more readily follow their leadership. What respect is communicated! What recognition and intrinsic value is bestowed!

As with God, so with his children: when communication is honest and continual and when it flows openly in both directions, all things go right.

Question No. 1: Why do we have to formalize private visits? Can't they grow normally out of everyday interaction?

Answer: Yes they can, and perhaps should, but do they? I find that in most busy, complicated family lives, they simply do not. We need to structure times for home evenings, family councils, family prayers, and private visits or they will simply be pushed aside by the heave and thrust of that which is structured—the tasks of life.

To adopt the practice of regular private visits is relatively easy with young children. They love the attention. With older children it is more difficult. Interaction patterns and defenses are more set. Having private visits with them may feel awkward at first, so a parent may need to start in a more natural way out of everyday activities and interactions.

It may take the commitment and determination of an upstream swimmer to regularly have one-to-one visits and to make them successful. But how they will pay off!

Question No. 2: Why should the youth control this particular private visit? Youth are already running too many homes. Don't they need to receive the direction and discipline of the parents more than ever today?

Answer: Yes, youth need and want direction and discipline. And considerable time, structured and unstructured, should be devoted to this. But there also needs to be some time given on a private basis for just listening, empathizing, supporting. If this becomes a time for lecturing or disciplining or parent-initiated advising, many young people will simply not open up. Then parents won't know their hearts.

They need to feel that "there is one time, one twenty-minute (or so) segment of the 168-hour week, that is completely mine. In it, Dad (or Mom) will listen and try to understand."

Such youth-centered visits will test our self-restraint and patience, but ironically they will also increase the positive influence of our teaching and disciplining at other times. Influence, like communication, is a two-way street.

"To every thing there is a season, and a time to every purpose under the heaven. . . . a time to keep silence, and a time to speak." (Eccl. 3:1, 7.)

IV

LEADERSHIP

28

Begin with the End in Mind

The scriptures teach us that the Lord created the world spiritually before he created it physically.

There is a profound, far-reaching principle here for parents, for leaders—in fact, for anyone who is serious in trying to accomplish anything.

The principle is: before you start an endeavor, form a clear picture of what you intend the outcome to be. Begin with the end in mind.

Whether making a cake or a dress, the housewife has the recipe or pattern in hand or in mind. She knows before she starts what she wants the cake to taste like or the dress to look like.

Before a building contractor puts a shovel into the ground, he has a detailed blueprint of the final product in hand. The intellectual creation comes first.

Before he takes up the baton, the great orchestra leader has an internal sense of the exact sounds he'll work for, of what the final outcome will be.

Yet for some reason most of us undertake many of our important personal family and occupational tasks without a clear outcome in mind. We focus on methods instead of results or objectives. In fact, gradually our methods often become our objectives.

To illustrate: a schoolteacher professes his major objective is to develop in his students the skill of problem solving and decision making (his intended outcome). Then he proceeds to do his favorite "thing"—lecturing.

Obviously his method, lecturing, won't achieve his objective. However good he may be as a lecturer, the development of the problem-solving/decision-making skill requires a method that dynamically involves the student in practicing the skill.

Another example is found in the mission field. The purpose or intended outcome of finding people is to teach them. However, if a missionary comes to think of tracting as his objective instead of as a method, he'll feel successful when he improves his tracting technique. He won't seriously consider other effective methods of finding people simply because, in his thinking, his method is his objective.

However, once this same missionary has a clear idea of his real objective, he will manifest amazing openness, ingenuity, and resourcefulness in achieving it.

There are several powerful advantages in first thinking results or objectives, then methods. Consider four:

1. When you know where you intend to end up, you know where you are now.

2. Knowing these two things, you have a .basis to make all the important decisions you will face. The prime one, of course, is how to get from where you are now to where you want to be. Results manage the choice and use of resources, methods, and procedures.

3. We effectively focus and unify our energies when we have gone through the very real struggle of mentally creating our desired outcome. Otherwise, with vague goals and superficial commitments, our efforts and attentions are scattered and diffused, easily distracted by external forces, internal disunity and weariness. Bogged down in details and crises, we're busy and active but not achieving.

Someone defined a fanatic as a person who, having lost sight of his destination, redoubled his speed. "I'm too busy preparing my lectures to ask why I lecture."

4. With clear, precise, strongly desired results in mind and relative freedom in method, almost unbelievable resources are released within us.

This way of thinking—begin with the end—is having a powerful influence today in industry (management by objectives, management by results, etc.) and in education (performance objectives, behavior objectives, individualized instruction, etc.)

Many believe our space effort really began to focus and accomplish when the vague, nebulous goal of 1957 to "achieve maximum capability in space" was changed in 1962 to the specific, measurable goal of "putting a man on the moon and returning him in safety by 1970."

The opportunities to apply this way of thinking in our personal and family lives and in our occupations are abundant, whether it be the character development of our children, or the development of creative home evenings, or doing results-oriented home teaching, or forming a successful business or whatever. In fact, if we choose, we can create each of our days in our minds and hearts before we live them in fact.

Private victories precede public victories.

29

Manage Time to Achieve Results

Some people accomplish so much more with the same time than others do. Why? Consider ten habits of effective time management. Observe how each focuses on thinking and acting in terms of objectives or results desired, rather than activities and procedures. None are sacred. All need adaptation to the circumstance.

1. ***The habit of setting clear, specific objectives in writing.***

When you have a clear, precise (writing brings precision) objective or desired outcome in mind, you become focused and effective in your energy output. Knowing where you're going, you know where you are and have a basis to evaluate methods and resources. You budget time accordingly.

2. ***The habit of carefully making plans to achieve specific objectives (measurable, if possible), including target dates.***

Those who do not hold planning time inviolate get bogged down in details. As Parkinson codified it, "Work expands to fill the time available for its completion."

3. ***The habit of doing first things first.***

Once an efficiency expert approached the president

of a large steel corporation and outlined his firm's services. "No use," the president responded, "I'm not managing as well as I know how now. We need action, not more knowing. If you could get us to do what we know we should, I'll pay you anything you ask."

"Fine," answered the consultant. "I can give you something in a few minutes to increase your doing and action fifty percent. First, write on a blank sheet the six most important tasks you have to do tomorrow. Second, put them in the order of their importance. Third, pull this sheet out the first thing tomorrow morning and begin working on item one. When you finish it, tackle item two, then item three. Do this until quitting time. Don't worry if you finish only two or three or even if you finish only one item. You'll be working on the most important ones. Fourth, take the last five minutes of each working day to make out a 'must' list for the next day's tasks."

Reportedly, the president sent the consultant $25,000 for the idea, $1,000 for each of the twenty-five minutes spent in the visit.

4. *The habit of doing creative and important personal communication work when most refreshed and doing routine and mechanical work when the fatigue level is higher.*

Most of us do the opposite. We do easy routine jobs when feeling good, "to get them out of the way," and procrastinate the more difficult, yet more important, jobs for later. But often, when later comes, fatigue has set in and the internal resources needed then are spent!

5. *The habit of doing paper work once, at your time, rather than continually going through an ever-mounting stack of bills, letters, notices, advertisements, and reading material.*

Such a paper shuffling process undermines confidence and feeds the spirit of guilt and procrastination and management by crisis. Instead, work to avoid touching paper or opening mail until you can take a specific action then and there, whether it is to answer or to pay or to file or to throw away or to defer for later action after mulling on it.

6. *The habit of holding effective meetings, characterized by a specific written purpose, an agenda sent out in sufficient time for individual preparation, and carefully recorded minutes (including assignments) sent out immediately.*

Then set up a simple assignment follow-up procedure so your program rewards results, not talk or busyness.

Many meetings simply don't need to be held. Careful planning, clear written communication, telephone visits or telephone conferences (three or more people hooked to the same circuit)—these can do away with many time-consuming meetings, particularly "emergency" types.

Also, start and stop meetings on time! It's amazing how such a practice, consistently followed, inspires a respect for everybody's time and eliminates irrelevant discussion.

7. *The habit of organizing healthy blocks of time for important creative work, such as planning or working on projects, and for vital communication or training work.*

These important endeavors require extended concentration and can't be effectively done here and there. By bunching less important meetings, appointments, phone calls, dictating, mechanical detail work, or whatever, we can budget large time chunks for the more important.

8. *The habit of taking time to get feedback on your communications.*

Perhaps nothing causes more frustration, bad feeling, and time wastage than unclear instructions or assignments. Are your ideas understood as you intended them to be? Test. Listen.

9. *The habit of taking time with your key people —understanding, delegating, committing, training, encouraging, appreciating.*

10. *The courage to say no to the unimportant.*

30

Keys to Effective Delegation

Delegation is the key to multiplying oneself. We delegate, of course, out of necessity: we simply have more work to do than we can do alone.

Let's examine the classic case of Moses and Jethro. Moses was killing himself off, trying to do everything for the children of Israel, to judge all matters, large and small. His father-in-law, Jethro, saw all this and advised, "The thing that thou doest is not good. Thou wilt surely wear away, both thou, and this people that is with thee: for this thing is too heavy for thee; thou art not able to perform it thyself alone."

Jethro then counseled Moses to do two things. First, Moses was to teach the people principles that embodied his judgments so they wouldn't have to come to him to decide every matter. They could reflect on the principles and think their problems through on their own. This is a powerful form of delegation—teaching true principles and trusting the people to apply them.

Second, Moses was to choose faithful followers and delegate all small matters to them, retaining to himself only matters of major importance.

Both of Jethro's recommendations required Moses to take more time at first in setting things up and to take risks. Instead of rendering judgments directly, he had to carefully select and train judges and put his faith in them. They might do it differently than he would. They might make mistakes.

However, Moses realized Jethro's counsel was right. The greater risks were *not* delegating. He delegated. (Study Exodus 18.)

Consider two reasons for not delegating: time and risk.

1. *Time*

Delegation does take more time in the beginning, and many who feel they are now pushed to the hilt simply won't take this time to explain, to train, to commit. Take the housewife who reasoned why she was still doing household tasks her children or other help could do: "I can do the job faster than it takes me to explain it. Besides, I do it better." Soon she accumulates so many things to do she feels even less time to delegate— to explain and train.

By analogy, her reasoning reminds me of the time I was too frantic picking up all my precious papers, which were blowing around my office, to take the time to close the window.

I'm convinced that we parents do many time-consuming tasks around the home that our children can and should do. But the time and process of identifying these tasks and of effectively training and committing our children to do them becomes the obstacle.

The initial delegating time spent, in the long run, is our greatest time saver.

2. *Risk*

To work through others involves the risk of doing things differently and sometimes doing things wrong. Often the top man in an organization, who is unwilling to delegate more than routine matters, has faith primarily in his own judgment and way of doing things. "It has brought me to where I am now. Why change? Why quarrel with success?" he reasons.

He has a point, and as long as he can continue successfully, we can't argue. Some people have extraordinary capacity and ability and can produce amazing results without delegating major responsibilities.

However, it somewhat depends on how we define success and results. Obviously people don't grow much as automatons, without solid responsibility for results and some freedom in method. In addition, organizations under such an arrangement are necessarily confined to the capacities of the top man. They reflect both his personal strength and weaknesses. To multiply oneself and to compensate for one's personal limitations require delegation.

The late J. C. Penney was quoted as saying that the wisest decision he ever made was to decide that he couldn't do it by himself any longer and that he had to let go. That decision, made long ago, enabled the development and growth of hundreds of stores and many thousands of individuals.

Many supervisors and organizations give lip service to the importance of delegation and development of people, but over a period of time, people learn otherwise. They learn to play it safe, to "make no waves." The politics of yesmanship and the art of mind-reading and second-guessing the boss are developed instead of resourcefulness and responsibleness.

Fearful of their boss and his autocratic, arbitrary ways, wanting everything done his way, they tell him what he likes to hear. Gradually, imperceptibly, he becomes insulated and isolated from what is really going on in the situation. His decisions and judgments suffer accordingly.

The boss didn't really want thinking, committed, responsible producers—he wanted carbon copies of himself. Consequently, the organization will perpetuate, not compensate for, his weaknesses and limitations. He also finds himself unable either to attract or to keep the very talented people he needs the most, unless they are rewarded in other ways.

In short, if we want responsible people and children, we must give them responsibility and hold them accountable. Consider the following simple four-step procedure in thinking through your own delegation opportunity:

1. Make a list of the tasks you do now.
2. Put them in the order of their importance.
3. Analyze each one. What is required to do it? Can it be delegated?
4. To whom? How? When?

Perhaps the crucial question is "If I delegate and trust another, am I willing to stick to my guns, to follow through?"

Delegation is the law of growth, both for organizations and for individuals. As with a child learning to walk, errors and mistakes are inevitably a part of the learning and growing process.

In the final analysis, effective delegation takes the emotional courage to allow, to one degree or another, others to make some mistakes on our own time, money, and good name. This courage consists of patience, self-control, faith in others and in their potential, and respect for individual differences.

31

Three Steps of Effective Delegation

Effective delegation is very much like effective communication. It must be two-way. A responsibility is given. A responsibility is received.

There are three distinct, yet interrelated, phases or steps in effectively delegating responsibility.

First, the initial agreement

This means both people have a clear understanding of what is expected and what resources, authority, latitude in method are given. This is the crucial step. It takes strong, clear thinking, a lot of two-way unguarded communication and commitment.

So far as practical, we should try to delegate by the results we expect of the person. Giving some freedom in method will help release the greatest potential in another. For when one is committed to results, he does what is necessary to achieve them. His creative potential is released. He'll grow the most with this approach, and so will the organization.

The typical delegating approach is to talk "duties" and "activities" and "time spent," which are methods in getting things done, not results.

The following are typical attitudes of people given responsibility for methods rather than results:

An employee: "I just knew it wouldn't work but he told me to do it that way. It's not my fault it didn't work out."

A daughter: "Mother won't like the way we do it anyway, so let's wait till she tells us what to do."

Whenever we delegate activities and specify all procedures, we retain responsibility for results ourselves. Perhaps this is the way we want it. That's fine, but let's not give the others the impression they're responsible for results or kid ourselves that we're effective motivators.

Rather, our attitude will likely become: "Unless I carefully follow through, I can't be certain the job will get done." Or we might even try to "hedge our bets": "Sometimes I even give two people the same job—unbeknown to each other—hoping at least one will come through."

When the expected results are obscure, neither person in the agreement knows how well things are going. Then, as with a vague legal contract, the likelihood of misunderstanding and personality conflicts are magnified many times.

Our real test in delegation comes when our employees or children do the job differently. If we think in terms of methods and procedures, to do things differently means to do things wrong. Then we can't bear to stand by and watch such mistakes, such neglect. So we step in.

When we step in and do the neglected work ourselves or have someone else do it; when we trounce someone for taking some initiative for doing it differently; when we double check everything and insist all decisions must be cleared; when we meticulously spell out every duty; when we overrule "their" decisions pertaining to "their" expected results; when we get rid of responsible yet independent thinkers and decision makers; when we multiply policies and procedures and rules—we take back responsibility.

And sometimes, in some situations, with some people, we should do this. But this is not delegating responsibility for results, and we'll need to provide closer, more time-consuming supervision to achieve them.

In short, we can't delegate results and supervise methods.

Second, the process of sustaining the delegatees (employee, child, etc.)

The original agreement of giving and receiving a responsibility immediately turns the supervisor into a source of help rather than of judgment and fear. As one effective executive put it, "I choose good men, give them the job, and then get out of their way."

The supervisor becomes their helping advocate, not their feared adversary. He provides resources. He removes obstacles. He sustains actions and decisions. He gives a vision—the big picture—and provides counsel and training when sought. He shares feedback in the form of information about results just as soon as it comes in.

Whenever the person falls down on the job, on the original agreement, this supervisor's attitude is "How can I help?" rather than "What's wrong with you?" It may be necessary to reaffirm the original agreement or to make out a new one.

Then who supervises? we ask. The delegatee is supervised by results, by actual performance. His conscience (sense of responsibility, commitment, and integrity) is enthroned, not his boss. And it is always with him. Generally a man who has a clear picture of exactly what's expected knows in his heart how he's doing better than his supervisor. This is one of the reasons, when vision and opportunity are given, why people set high goals for themselves and are more strict in evaluating their own work than others would dare be.

Third, the accountability process

The "days of judgment" are based on the original agreement or contract. It is largely one of self-evaluation, since result information was given as soon as it was available. This is also an ideal time to revise objectives and plans in terms of the current situation to challenge, to commit, to inspire, to appreciate.

There is no need to "fire" people with this delegation process. People are dignified throughout and will resign themselves or seek a new assignment, training, or special help to make them equal to their present one.

In contrast to the traditional approach, in which the supervisor evaluates and motivates, the follow-up process in this approach is always in terms of the original agreement. The delegatee evaluates and motivates himself. What time it saves! What human potential is released!

The key throughout this entire three-step process for the delegator—whether parent or supervisor—is to think clearly and to be strong and consistent within himself.

32

The Best Way to Learn Is by Doing

The only way to learn how to play tennis is by playing it. Hearing about it, reading about it, watching others play it will help teach good theory, but good skill is developed only in practice.

This idea holds not only in the world of sports but also in less obvious areas of life, in developing true skill and competence in anything, whether it be how to give an understanding response, how to resolve conflict, or how to courageously confront another with certain realities.

Two principles of learning are involved. First, we learn *what* to do by listening, reading, watching, etc. Second, we learn *how* to do by doing, by practicing the *what*.

What to do and how to do it are two different kinds of knowledge and are frequently confused. Each kind of knowledge is vital and complements the other. One cannot be substituted for the other. Neither can one stand alone. For effectiveness, they depend upon each other.

What-to-do knowledge might be called intellectual or mind knowledge. How-to-do-it knowledge might be called instinctive, habit, or nerve-fiber knowledge.

Let me illustrate.

A mission president determined to teach the district and branch presidents how to give a call. He believed that if the calls were given correctly, resulting in a deep commitment, a fundamental cause of many problems would be eliminated.

The training meeting dealt with the great importance of giving a call right and with fundamental principles in doing so.

What happened? Some momentary inspiration and resolution. But shortly the leaders dropped back to their old ways and habits.

The leader then decided the district and branch presidents needed a second session to "see" the principles demonstrated.

Result? Again very little, if any, change. He wrongly assumed learning plus seeing would do the trick. He had again taught the "what" but not the "how." They were reconvinced but not converted, not changed. How to give a call is a skill, like tennis, and is learned best by doing.

Thus, the third training session provided opportunity for each person to practice giving calls, utilizing where appropriate the principles. They practiced all day—giving several calls, to different people, in differing circumstances. After each practice they'd get feedback from both an observer and the one receiving the call. Then they'd practice again. Then more feedback and theory. Then more practice in light of it. Then reflect. Then practice.

Something very basic was beginning to happen. Knowledge was becoming skill and their success thrilled them. They left that day fatigued but converted and happy. The effect in the mission was immediate in most areas. The leaders enthusiastically reported the results of giving calls right, both on themselves and with their people. Success bred more success.

Consider two additional implications for all of us who are interested in improving our own human skills and in helping others improve theirs.

First, learning by doing, however vital, is difficult. It obviously seems less efficient than telling or showing. It takes more time, more patience, more courage.

It usually involves an awkward phase of unlearning for many adults. Like trying to learn the right tennis grip, after years of doing it wrong, you don't know where you are for a while. It's uncomfortable. Sometimes it's downright embarrassing.

Second, when possible, it's best to practice in an environment that makes it easy and rewarding to learn from mistakes. You wouldn't practice your new tennis grip for the first time in a tournament.

I find most people are in this very dilemma in life: they know what to do but not how to do it. And they're afraid to go through the inevitably awkward mistake-making process of learning *how* for fear of embarrassment or ridicule. The guilt resulting from this "knowledge gap" is often crippling—unnecessarily.

A gentle home is an ideal place to learn human skills. Husbands and wives can even role play with each other how to communicate with their children on sensitive issues. The priceless skill of empathy is thus sharpened. Leaders and teachers can also design training programs that include opportunity for practice and for feedback.

When you think deeply about it, from an eternal perspective the principle of learning by doing is the essence of our purpose in mortality.

33

Integrity:
The Foundation of Leadership

A great deal is heard nowadays of the credibility gap. It's another way of saying: "Are they giving us the straight scoop?" "Can we trust them?"

These questions are felt, if not asked, everywhere— children ask of their parents, employees of their bosses, church workers of their leaders.

All of this inward doubting and questioning underscores the most fundamental but often neglected (with so much emphasis on technique, knowledge, style) principle of successful leadership: that the character or integrity of the leader is supreme.

The Lord gives a magnificent illustration of this as he contrasts three different leadership and teaching types or methods. Study the chart below in relation to John 10:1-15.

First note that since the shepherd (No. 1) truly cares for the sheep, he can be open and honest in communicating with them. He has no need to pretend or to manipulate from a distance. With pure motives, the sheep trust him and will also be open with him; thus, two-way communication. He has listened and understands their hopes and fears and needs. They know he cares, for he is kind and is willing to sacrifice himself for them. Therefore, he can lead them from in front through the drawing power of example and love. They give their loyalty, co-operation, and best effort. And their common goals are achieved.

But the hired sheepherder, a hireling (No. 2), has no such character. He's in it for his wage, whether it be money or power or even a better job, with more prestige. However, to win approval and to make good impressions, he pretends to care. Sometimes he professes his sincere intentions most vigorously. But since attitude communicates more eloquently than words, the sheep are puzzled. The trumpet isn't giving forth a certain sound. ("White man speaks with forked tongue.")

Consequently he can't lead in front. They won't follow. So he drives from behind and uses one approach after another to keep them moving or working. Carrot (reward) and stick (threats), hovering over, lecturing, "psyche up" cheerleading meetings, and other manipulations, such as buttering 'em up, chewing 'em out.

He doesn't need to wonder why attendance is low, why meetings and activities lack punch, why loyalty is superficial. "A double minded man is unstable in all his ways." (James 1:8.)

When the going really gets rough, when "the wolf" comes, his real motives surface. He deserts the sheep. He gives up on that ungrateful, rebellious son. He asks the bishop for a release or another job—and, of course, he has a "good" reason.

But sometimes he just resigns inside and grows indifferent and goes through the motions, like the sheep-type leader.

The sheep leader (No. 3) wants to be liked by everybody. He's often socially intelligent, knowing what others want, but has no vision or lifting power. He compromises the program, even the standards. His children and those he supervises like all the good and fun times—the course of least resistance—but when the going gets rough he can't understand why they desert him and follow a stronger-minded sheep.

Far and away the most important factor in leadership is the depth of sincere care in the leader. If we don't really care, all the latest techniques and leadership formulas will bring failure. But with it we can have success in spite of some bungling. As someone once put it, "I don't care how much you know until I know how much you care."

To become shepherds we must follow the True Shepherd.

TYPE OF LEADERSHIP

	1. Shepherd	2. Hired Sheepherder (Hireling)	3. Sheep
Character Motive	Love of sheep (people being supervised)	Love of wage ("What's in it for me?", glory, etc.)	Safety, security, belonging
Communication	Honest ("for they know his voice") Two-way: ("and am known of mine")	Dishonest, disguised ("know not the voice of strangers") One-way: his way or downward	Self-concerned, One-way
Leadership	Leads in front by example and love	Drive from behind— carrot (rewards) and stick (threats) approach. Hovering supervision	Follow—no vision, no drive, just go along like a "good guy"
Consequences	Safety, loyalty, self-realization, achievement of goals	Sheep deserted (resigns, is indifferent) when times get rough (when wolf approaches)	Course of least resistance; a Judas sheep could lead them astray

V

GENERAL
PRINCIPLES

34

Understanding Our Problems

What are your problems?

A problem that can be understood is half solved. Consider three steps in understanding your problems.

First, think deeply about the problems that concern you most. What are they? Personal problems, such as a big career decision or the habit of procrastination? Family problems, such as improving your communication with your spouse or child? Financial problems, such as meeting payments or how to get ahead and save for college and missions?

Church problems, such as how to get people out to meeting, how to internally motivate the home teachers, how to get the priesthood leader to understand the needs of your auxiliary, how to release someone without offending them?

Work problems, such as how to get the ear of the boss, or how to secure more cooperation and dedication from your employees?

Or how to do all your church jobs without neglecting your family? How to handle rebellious teenagers? How to reach or reactivate an indifferent family member?

Second, classify all your problems under one of three categories: (1) direct control (own behavior, attitudes, decisions); (2) indirect control (others' behavior, attitudes, decisions); (3) no control (the past, natural laws and forces, certain fixed realities you live in).

This second step will take careful thinking and you may be amazed, if not chagrined, to find that you have no control whatever over many of your concerns and problems. Furthermore, you may have unwittingly acted on the assumption in the past that, in the name of position or authority or money, you could directly influence or control the behavior of others.

Perhaps you can buy a man's time, physical presence, or even his skill to do a particular job. You can almost force or pressure an employee or a young person to conform. But you cannot buy cooperation, you cannot buy loyalty, you cannot buy enthusiasm or initiative or resourcefulness. You cannot buy the dedication of heart, mind, and soul. You have to earn these things.

This is why some of us have been frustrated in the past; knowingly or unknowingly, we have assumed that indirect control problems were under our direct control.

Third, by using the same three categories, decide on a plan of action to deal with or solve the problems. In this process you'll discover one very simple, yet profound, truth. The answer to any of your problems lies in changing yourself.

Let me illustrate.

With regard to direct control problems—your own behavior—this truth is self-evident. If your problem is weight, you can immediately begin a regimen of dieting and/or exercise to solve it. If your problem is lack of ability to communicate, you can begin to take steps, such as acquire training, to overcome it. In short, direct control problems are solved by changing your habits of doing and thinking; in other words, self-control.

What about indirect control problems? You say, "Why must I change when it's my wife's (or husband's or child's or boss's) fault?" Simply because your past methods of influence haven't worked. If they had worked, you wouldn't have the problem, would you? Since they didn't work, you had better use new methods of influencing others. And this means you will have to change. You need to change your methods of influence, which means changing your own doing and thinking behavior. Again, self-control.

For instance, we all hear complaints from time to time that "if only the boss could understand my program or my problem. . . ." But few complainers take the time to prepare the kind of presentation that the boss would listen to and respect, in his language, with his problems in mind.

Now take the last category—no control problems. Since we can't control the problems, we can control our reaction to them. We decide within ourself how anything or anybody outside ourself will affect us. This attitude control frees one from circumstances and the judgments of others. We can learn from failures; develop patience and courage from trying situations; radiate cheer and hope in suffering. Our Lord is the supreme exemplar of this kind of overcoming, this self-control.

The great psychologist-philosopher William James put it: "The greatest single discovery of my generation is that we can change our circumstances by a mere change of our attitude."

We must look to ourselves for solutions.

"Keep thy heart with all diligence; for out of it are the issues of life." (Proverbs 4:23.)

35

Keep Means and Ends Straight

It was going to be the best trip the family had ever taken—and the best vacation too. They were going east. A whole month's trip!

Oh, how thrilled the parents were, especially for their children! When they were young they had never had such a privilege. "Just think, kids," they would enthusiastically say, "to see the very birthplaces of our church and our country. When you visit the Sacred Grove and the Hill Cumorah you'll come to appreciate the truth and value of the Church just as we do."

At first the children were excited, but gradually, beginning with the teenagers, they grew indifferent and apathetic toward the trip and, at times, even resentful. They began to moan about having to leave their friends and all the summer fun on the social agenda.

The parents were both hurt and puzzled by this reaction. They had saved and prepared so long and held such high educational and spiritual expectations for such a trip! Now the children seemed so ungrateful, so unaware, so self-centered.

With the trip still weeks away, they were about to call the whole thing off when they discussed the situation with a friend who wasn't so emotionally involved.

This friend observed that the children might be reacting against the feeling that more value was being attached to the marvelous trip than was being given to them. "They may also be reacting against the fear of not being able to meet your high learning expectations."

A fear of failure, particularly of becoming unacceptable through it, destroys the very desire to try. Many people fear success for a similar reason: one success creates the expectation of more, which means more pressure and possible disappointment.

The friend suggested the parents stop pushing the trip and talking out *their* excitements and expectations. "Just live naturally and cheerfully, leave travel brochures and material about, and let the children express themselves as they naturally desire to. Don't judge their expressions; just listen to them. Listen to *their* interests, *their* enthusiasms, what *they* are looking to. Give value to your children rather than to the trip."

The parents did this and within a short time the children were all fired up about the trip. No one could talk about anything else, right up to departure time.

And the trip surpassed everybody's expectations!

This little family episode illustrates how easy it is to confuse means—methods and experiences—and ends, or ultimate purposes and values. These parents had placed more value on what they wanted their children to learn than on the children themselves. The children sensed this and rebelled by going in the very opposite direction, almost as if to test whether the parents put any value on them as they were. Once they felt assured of intrinsic worth and of their parents' unconditional love for them, they were freed of the need or desire to rebel. They were acceptable as they were and therefore could take on this new adventure without fear of becoming unacceptable if certain expectations were not realized.

But when we show respect only for certain *shoulds* of life and condition our love on conformity to these *shoulds*, we have a reactive, negative influence. Youth often then rebel against the very thing we're trying to teach under the popular, although defensive, banner "I gotta be me."

We have all seen people almost reactively driven into bad attitudes, bad experiences, even bad marriages, by well-intentioned but unwise parents who confuse ends and means by communicating conditional love and acceptance.

I saw this in myself just the other day in as small a thing as trying to teach my little son to swim. Placing more value on his swimming than on him—his level, interests, fears, and feelings—I found myself almost forcing through shame and comparison, through subtle threats and conditional love. Result? Hurt feelings and an aversion toward swimming in spite of my repentance.

The supreme value is the individual personality. Its growth and development according to the gospel plan is the supreme purpose. Everything else is a means to that end.

Outside of example—love's expression—nothing encourages a person to obey the sacred principles and laws of life more than our obedience to the laws of love toward that person.

36

We Reap Only What We Sow

Hearing a knock at the door, I opened it and invited Clyde, a student of mine, in.

"I've come to find out how I'm doing in your class," he commented.

I had sensed a tendency to just get by in Clyde since the beginning of the term, and from other contacts we developed a good rapport together, so I felt safe in confronting him directly.

"Clyde, you really know how you're doing far better than I do. You didn't really come in to find out how you're doing but rather to find out how I thought you were doing, to see if you were 'beating the system.' You tell me, Clyde, just how are you doing?"

"Not very well," he answered. "I really haven't been able to put the time in I should have. I have such a heavy load and have been so busy with school activities."

I continued to confront him. "Clyde, aren't these just excuses for your own laziness in getting down to your studies as you should?"

He then opened up and admitted he'd been goofing off and that it was getting so late in the term he was beginning to worry and was now attempting to find out how he stood with each teacher so he could intelligently begin the cramming process.

The practice of "psyching out" the teacher, figuring out what he wants, how he tests, what one has to do and doesn't have to do, develops the attitudes of second guessing, masterminding, and appearing to be, as well as the skills of memorizing, regurgitating, and forgetting. As one student put it, "I don't work to learn. I just work to get good grades."

These tendencies are widespread not just with the youth in school today but with all age levels in all fields of endeavor. Consider your own past school experiences and habits, and you may find you too had these tendencies. I did.

The problem is that this approach in many social or manmade systems works. Some cramming experts learn to get by well in school without really learning how to think, to work, to communicate, to cooperate. Many whose personal and family lives are pockmarked with inconsideration, irresponsibility, and selfishness learn how to wear a different mask for the public and make quite an impression. They are successful for a while, but constant role playing is tortuous and fatiguing, and sooner or later a stress or dilemma situation will shear away their false facade, revealing the hypocrisy underneath. Justice is an exact taskmaster, and all accounts are eventually paid to him in full.

Even in church work we can strive for appearances of activity and faithfulness, so as to impress others, while inside we know we are not magnifying or being magnified.

Although its harvest in the long run is bitter, this shortcut approach is powerfully appealing, for it excuses consistent personal effort, initiative, and responsibility. Manmade religious doctrines of salvation are built upon it. Economic and political philosophies revolve around it.

I believe the key for parents, teachers, and leaders in resisting such shortcut doctrines and cramming practices is found in studying natural or God-made systems, as opposed to those that are social or manmade.

Take farming, for instance. Can you imagine a farmer cramming to bring in the harvest? You know, forgetting to plant in the spring, throwing some seed out in the summer, neglecting the weeding and watering, and then just before the big harvest really hitting it in an all-night session?

Can you imagine a mile runner, competing in the Olympics, cramming? Even though he looked great at the gun, within a lap the months of dissipation and violated training rules would show in his lungs and legs.

This means to raise your young with increasing amounts of real responsibility for results, where results can be seen, if possible. No escapes. No excuses. Appearances only are unacceptable.

This means to patiently teach and train them in the law of the harvest: we reap only what we sow. Then we must commit them, followed by showing trust in asking them to judge their own effort and performance, in terms of their consciences, their trained sense of responsibility. My experience convinces me that if we are honest and genuinely care, they will tell us how they are really doing and they will often ask for our help rather than pretending everything's okay.

This means we will also need to get close enough to them to do some honest confronting and to give candid feedback. We will need courage to keep from shielding them from the consequences of their actions and attitudes, particularly when some of those consequences might embarrass us.

Obviously to try to teach and do these things when we ourselves live by appearances, cramming, and shortcuts is like playing golf with a tennis racket.

37

Accept in Order to Improve

One of the most common hangups people face in solving human problems is their own inability or unwillingness to face present realities. They refuse to start working on the situation as it is. They want it the way they want it or the way it should be.

To avoid facing and dealing with present facts is as foolish as a father saying to his son, "I don't care if the doctor says you've got rickets. You look perfectly healthy to me. Get up and do your work!" The very first step in that son's recovery is for both father and son to accept the fact that the boy has rickets! The next step is to begin to do something about it. But unless the first is taken, the next will never follow.

Take a wife, for instance, who constantly badgers and nags her husband to change. She refuses to accept him the way he is. "Of course I refuse!" she exclaims. "That's not how he should be! If I accept him, he'll never change."

However ironical it may seem, the first step in changing or improving another is to accept him as he is. Similarly, nothing reinforces present defensive behavior more than judgment or rejection.

Why is this so? First, simply because to be accepted is deeply satisfying and to be rejected is deeply threatening—like being eliminated from the human race. (One father actually told his asthmatic daughter to "leave the room if you have to breathe that way.") And second, because a feeling of acceptance and worth frees a person from the need to defend and helps release the natural growth tendency to improve.

Acceptance is not condoning a weakness or agreeing with an opinion. Rather, it is affirming the intrinsic worth of another through admitting or acknowledging that he does feel or think a particular way.

The apostle Peter, in substance, counseled, "Wives, if you have 'the word' and your husbands have not 'the word' and you want to bring your husbands to 'the word,' then do it without the use of 'the word.' Do it by your good behavior and by the unfailing loveliness of a meek and gentle spirit." (See 1 Peter 3.)

Many a wife or husband has seen miracles gradually happen in their homes once they stopped trying to reform their spouses and began to work upon themselves so as to be a light rather than a judge.

Look to your children for abundant evidence of the power of acceptance. Just recently I saw it in my six-year-old son as he learned to catch a baseball. At first he refused to play with the older children. He said he didn't care to play, that he wanted to do other things. The other things essentially amounted to spying on the others out of the corner of his eye. Actually, the problem was that he cared too much. The possible hurt and embarrassment of failure, of not being able to catch, outweighed the enjoyment of learning.

Then I saw my teenage daughter take him aside and let him know she accepted him and accepted the fact he didn't know how to catch very well but that she would teach him how to catch if he wanted her to. He did. Acceptance punctured the fear and sting of failure; in fact, it redefined it as a kind of success. Success is often on the far side of failure.

Consider three additional reasons why we often hold

back from accepting another or agreeing to begin working with the situation as it is.

First, it is so much easier to reject and judge than to accept and understand. It takes so little effort to preach the *shoulds* and so much patience and courage to deal with the knotty or the unpleasantness of what is.

Second, we think accepting certain realities is negative. To think positively is not to reject or deny certain seen realities but rather to accept them and then to believe in the unseen realities (the potential within), and to act accordingly. Our attitude can be "I accept you as you are but I treat you as you can and should be." For what a person is includes what he can become.

Few things are more negative and frustrating than that brand of positive thinking which denies the existence of things as they are and finds itself unable to give straight answers to simple questions.

Third, to accept another and to willingly and patiently work within the present situation, beginning at the present level, takes self-acceptance. This, in turn, emerges from honest self-communication and searching. This may be agonizing, for accepting another as he or she is now may make us feel responsible and guilty for the unhappy consequences of failure to do so in the past.

As it is put in boxing lingo, "You have to hit from where your fist is."

38

Mercy Must Not Rob Justice

It was the night before the last day of finals. I could hear someone opening drawers and files in the office of another professor who I knew was out of town. A student shortly came out and explained to me he was turning in some late papers and had found the door unlocked.

After some checking about I was convinced this student had stolen the final exam, but the nature of the evidence was such that I would have to involve the other professor to clearly establish proof. I hesitated to do this, for I knew the teacher would immediately flunk the student. There would be no mercy. The student needed the class for graduation, which was to take place the next day. The student's parents and family had traveled a considerable distance to participate in all the final festivities and to see him graduate. He had his job lined up and was to start within a month. He was a very prominent school officer. On and on I reasoned with myself.

I decided to confront him directly rather than involve his professor. He denied everything and explained away all the circumstantial evidence I presented.

Again I debated within myself, finally deciding to let him know that I knew he had cheated but would not involve his professor because I felt the consequences on so many people would exceed his terrible wrong.

Almost a year later I asked an officer of the company he hired with how he was getting along.

"He's now with another company," was the answer.

"Why, what happened?" I inquired.

After pressing a little more, this company official said, "We have enough on him to send him to the federal penitentiary for five years." And then he gave the history: how outstanding his first months were—so outstanding they took a deep look and found all kinds of wheeling and dealing, some illegal, much borderline.

"Why didn't you confront him with the law?" I asked.

"We were afraid of the consequences. His parents, family—so many were involved."

How those words pierced my conscience! I wondered how much guilt was mine for letting "mercy rob justice." In fact, I found that this individual had a consistent pattern of getting away with things for years. He was able to talk himself out of almost everything. There was always an escape. A smooth talker, popular with many, trusted by none. Several of us, through his formative years, could see this pattern evolving and could have done something about it, could have faced him up to the real consequences of his own actions.

The cancerous spirit of lawlessness afflicting our nation today also had small beginnings. We can do something about the seeds we sow and how we tend them, but nothing about the harvest we reap. We have no control over consequences, only over actions and attitudes.

One of the kindest things, therefore, we can do for our children is to let the natural or logical consequences of their own actions teach them responsible behavior, justice. They may not like it or us, but popularity is a fickle standard by which to measure character development. Only sincere repentance, not mercy, can satisfy the demands of justice. (Study Alma 42.)

Insisting on justice demands more true love, not less. We care enough for their growth and security to suffer their displeasure. It is at this time, or shortly after their negative emotions spend themselves, that we need to "show forth an increase of love." They learn that law governs life and that we ourselves can be depended upon to be faithful to that law.

Whenever we, as parents or teachers or leaders, see a pattern of lawlessness or phoniness developing in our young people, then is the time to do some serious one-to-one teaching. Often, however, talking isn't enough; it may be *their* long suit. We need to clearly point out exactly what the consequences are if things continue. Then our consistent, kind-but-firm follow-through will eloquently communicate our sincerity and serious purpose.

Just as shock treatments help bring some highly disturbed people back to reality, so does candidly confronting someone we are responsible to, that we see through their phoniness, that we care enough for them to not let them get by with it anymore, and that we believe in them enough to expect more.

A life of pretense is so tortuous many literally hunger to be released from it by someone who they know "sees through me," who "understands me," and most importantly, who "cares enough to stay with me on the road back."

39

The Need for Meaningful Projects

He was a restless boy. Irritable, too—always picking fights with younger brothers and sisters. He was uncooperative and bored. You could tell he was unhappy.

This teenager's parents were almost beside themselves trying to get him to change.

But through honest introspection and prayer, the parents eventually got a grip on themselves and refused to be controlled any longer by the spirit that he brought to the home. Then one day the father noticed, and was surprised by, his son's interest in some sketchy plans for a fence around the yard. He quickly seized the opportunity to involve his son. Little by little the boy became so involved in planning the project that he wanted to build it himself.

And build it he did. It took him several hours every day for over two months. He made a lot of mistakes—his father let him. But the final product was beautiful. And what a transformation in the attitude of the boy and in the spirit of the home! What a sense of achievement all around!

Just as soon as the teenage son found a meaningful project and reacted responsibly to it, all his energies were unified and focused. Reaping an inner sense of purpose and fulfillment, he lost the need to take his inner void and conflict out on others.

This story illustrates the healing influence of a meaningful project and implies two principles.

First, what is meaningful to a parent may be meaningless to a child. In addition to teaching values, we need to empathize with and show respect for the child's own interests and then to create opportunities for developing them.

Second, projects take on meaning when people are involved in the planning and thinking processes. Your thinking and my doing aren't nearly as involving or exciting as my (or our) thinking and my (or our) doing.

The story also involves an even more basic principle of life with much wider application, one that applies to all of us. It is the supreme importance of having a sense of meaning or purpose in our daily activities.

Dr. Viktor E. Frankl, president of the Austrian Medical Society for Psychotherapy, is the father of a fascinating philosophy based on every person's need for a sense of meaning, called logotherapy.

He developed logotherapy out of harrowing years in Nazi prison camps during World War II. He learned what he called "the last of human freedoms"—the ability to choose one's attitudes in a given set of circumstances.

A doctor primarily deals with problems or diseases originating or manifested in the body. The psychotherapist is primarily concerned with mental and emotional illnesses. Inevitably, both the doctor and the therapist deal extensively with psychosomatic illnesses, those having to do with the intimate relationship between mind and body.

Logotherapy concerns itself with the relationship between mind and spirit, teaching that many mental/ emotional illnesses or neuroses are caused by a sense of meaninglessness, a sense of inner emptiness, a spiritual void. In short, many so-called mental and emotional illnesses are really symptoms of spiritual sickness.

Logotherapy attempts to eliminate this sickness, this emptiness, by helping the individual to detect, not invent, his unique meaning in life, even in suffering. How encouraging it is to find a therapy that attempts to deal with the whole of man's personality, particularly that spiritual dimension which is filled with meaning and potential and with a consciousness of responsibility.

All people need to be "anxiously engaged in a good cause." Without such projects, life loses its meaning and we wither and die before our time. The life-span of people who retire, looking for a tensionless state, without meaningful projects, is short. Dr. Frankl found that when prisoners lost a sense of hope and meaning, they gave up their will to live and they died.

Life is actually sustained by tension between where we are now and some goal out there worth straining and struggling for.

This kind of goal tension is fundamentally different from that kind of dissipating tension which emerges from conflicting motives and desires, from trying to be all things to all people, from hectic pressurized schedules, and from immersion in, as one put it, "the thick of think things."

Instead of asking what the meaning of life is, in the abstract sense, we need to ask, "What is life asking of me in this situation?" We then give our answer to life (conscience) by reacting responsibly in that situation. Responsibleness is the essence of mental health and happiness.

This whole idea, and much more, is best expressed in the incomparable philosophy of the Savior. "He who loses his life for my sake shall find it."

40

Seven Final Convictions

I would like to share seven of my deepest convictions regarding human and family relations.

1. If asked what the single most helpful principle in this area is, I would answer: seek first to understand, then to be understood.

Most of us do the very opposite. We want to be first understood. For example, take a parent who says, "How can I reach my teenagers? They won't listen to me at all!"

Examine this puzzled father's expression again. I suggest the declaration "They won't listen to me at all" is the answer to his opening question "How can I reach my teenagers?" This father feels sure he's right in what he wants to tell his children—and he probably is—but, like it or not, in order to reach his teenage children, he may have to listen to them first before they will listen to him.

Often when we do listen we're too like the rushed driver at a red light. We anxiously wait for the green light so we can go, so we can have our say, so we can be understood. We simply aren't listening—we only stop talking and prepare our next response.

We must diagnose (understand) before we prescribe (advise).

2. The second principle builds naturally on the first: we have influence with others to the degree they feel they have influence with us.

When another feels you genuinely care about him and that you understand his unique problems and feelings, he also feels he has influenced you. He will then become amazingly open to your influence.

We take the prescription *because* it is based on the diagnosis.

3. We best encourage obedience to the laws of life when we live the laws of love.

People are extremely tender inside, particularly those who act as if they are not, and very often those we think self-sufficient. And if we'll listen carefully with the third ear, the heart, they'll tell us so.

The key to people lies in showing love, particularly unconditional love. This is a basic kind of love that gives people a sense of intrinsic worth and security. It is unrelated to conforming behavior or comparison with others. Many have never experienced it in their upbringing, and they live out of internal doubt and fear. They therefore borrow their security and strength from external things— appearances, status symbols, authoritative positions, past achievements, associations.

This pattern passes from generation to generation, for borrowing strength inevitably builds weakness. "Only by persuasion, by long-suffering, by gentleness and meekness, and by love unfeigned. . . ."

A love-starved child is as incapable of truly responsible behavior as a cripple is of winning foot races. One little act of kindness, one effort to understand, will do more to win cooperation and confidence than a thousand logical lectures. Such pure love is magic and will work miracles in reforming lives.

We all distrust superficial human relations techniques and manipulative success formulas that do not flow out of a sincere attitude and a character of integrity. Over time they boomerang. "Though I speak with the tongues of men and of angels, and have not charity, I am become as sounding brass, or a tinkling cymbal." (1 Corinthians 13:1.)

4. There is a redeeming power that can make up for deficiencies in our upbringing and that can enable us to overcome our most deeply ingrained habits and tendencies. The world knows little about this power source—and science, nothing.

The statement "the child is always father of the man" means that the first few years of childhood so structure the character as to last a lifetime. Such widely believed determinism may have some validity except for the power of the Savior who gives, to those who will receive him in the revealed way, a new birth, a new childhood, a divine nature.

There is no other way to change man's nature, to purify his heart. Legislation won't do it. Education won't do it. Believing repentance unto Christ will.

5. We can't walk crooked and think straight.

Those who have entered into gospel covenants are under a different set of laws and expectations—a different psychology, if you will—than those who do not. The mental and emotional consequences of disobedience are more severe and are infinitely more sublime to the faithful. Gospel therapy alone can heal the sick soul or the broken relationship. Such therapy embraces the true principles and methods in every other therapy and, in addition, embodies the transcendent power of the Savior.

Because the root of our problems is spiritual, the root solution must be also.

6. There is no shortcut in building a victorious personality or a beautiful relationship or an eternal family. God's law of the harvest governs—we reap as we sow.

Growth, therefore, is a step-by-step process. It can't be skipped, forced, or feigned. Through diligent obedience to the right laws it can be accelerated. But expecting perfection before sundown is sure discouragement, like trying to do calculus without understanding algebra. We must simply do some things before we can do other things.

The common thread, therefore, that interweaves itself through success in every department of life is self-discipline. Our flesh must increasingly become a servant of our spirit and our spirit a servant of the Holy Spirit.

7. Finally, to do all the rest, we must never become too busy to sharpen the saw. This means to regularly exercise and tune the three instruments we have to do our work—our body, our mind, and our spirit.

The center of the spiritual exercise is two-way prayer, which involves listening with the heart to the still small voice of the Spirit and then committing to obey what is heard. The Lord often awaits our answer before he will give his.

Such a daily private victory is the key to all other victories.

INDEX